FAQ

FREQUENTLY ASKED

QUESTIONS ABOUT

the CHRISTIAN LIFE

RAY PRITCHARD

FAQ

FREQUENTLY ASKED

QUESTIONS ABOUT

the CHRISTIAN LIFE

BROADMAN
& HOLMAN
PUBLISHERS

Nashville, Tennessee

0–8054–2340–0

Published by Broadman & Holman Publishers,
Nashville, Tennessee

Dewey Decimal Classification: 230
Subject Heading: CHRISTIAN LIVING

Unless otherwise noted, Scripture quotations are from the Holy Bible,
New International Version, © copyright 1973, 1978, 1984.

Library of Congress Cataloging-in-Publication Data

Pritchard, Ray, 1952–
Frequently asked questions : about the Christian life. / Ray Pritchard.
p. cm.
ISBN 0–8054–2340–0
1. Theology, Doctrinal—Popular works. 2. Christian life.V
I. Title: Frequently asked questions. II. Title.

BT77 .P744 2001
230—dc21

2001035748

1 2 3 4 5 6 7 8 9 10 05 04 03 02 01

To
Glen and Mia Gale
and
Davis and Kathy Duggins
Trusted colleagues
Beloved friends
With gratitude and much affection

CONTENTS

INTRODUCTION

It is sometimes said that preachers answer questions that no one is asking. Several years ago I decided to tackle that problem head-on by asking my congregation to submit a list of questions they would like answered from the pulpit. To my surprise (and delight) we received more than six hundred questions covering virtually every area of theology, Bible knowledge, and the spiritual life. Since they came from the congregation at large and were unsigned, they ran the gamut from detailed theology ("Why is the Trinity so important?") to straight Bible questions ("What does Hebrews 6:4–6 really mean?") to questions about specific doctrine ("Can I lose my salvation?") to questions about controversial issues ("Can a Christian believe in evolution?").

Many questions tugged at the heart, such as "My parents fight all the time. What can I do about it?" and "How can I raise teenagers who love the Lord?" There were questions from people who were clearly searching for the Lord and the occasional unusual query about UFOs and the Bible. A few questions were of the "angels on the head of a pin" variety, but most were very practical.

Out of that survey came a sermon series in which I attempted to answer the most important questions. Not long after that I was asked to be an occasional guest host on a national radio call-in program. On those broadcasts I talk to listeners scattered across America and (via the Internet) around the world. Many of the questions touch on the need for very basic instruction in the Christian faith. Most people have sincere questions about troubling Bible passages or ask for help with things like prayer, temptation, and knowing God's will.

From listening to my own congregation and by talking with people on the air, I have put together the most important questions in an easy-to-read format. You need to know right up front that I believe the Bible is the Word of God and is, therefore, the only reliable source for answering the greatest questions of life. The Bible does not tell us everything we could know on every subject, but it tells us everything we need to know about who God is and how we can live in a way that pleases him. We need to hear what he has to say.

I wrote this book for new believers, young Christians (both in age and in years knowing the Lord), and for any church member who needs a refresher course in the Christian faith. It helps to remember that coming to Christ is not like taking up a new hobby. Becoming a Christian means taking a journey that starts on earth and ends in heaven. Each chapter of this book will help you stay on course as a Christian.

The first chapter discusses the difference between a religious person and someone who is truly born again. The next few chapters discuss eternal security, the kind of church you should join, the filling of the Spirit, knowing God's will, and how to pray. Then there are chapters on temptation, suffering, spiritual warfare, and sharing your faith. The final three chapters move into the future as we discuss death, heaven, and the second coming of Christ.

No single book can answer all your questions. There is much more to learn about spiritual disciplines, Bible doctrine, and how to handle your daily problems. But this book will help you get grounded in your faith. It's like basic training in the military. In these pages you'll learn vital information that prepares you for the next step in your walk with the Lord.

Two final words: First, I hope you won't read this book straight through. You can do that, of course, but most people will gain more by reading a little bit at a time. You may want to use it as part of your daily quiet time with the Lord, or you might enjoy reading it as part of a small group Bible study or a Sunday school class. I think you'll probably grow faster if you study it with other Christians who are also committed to spiritual growth. Feel free to underline the text and to jot down questions in the margin. This is *your* book and I want it to help *you*. Second, each of the thirteen chapters deals with one major question. And each chapter ends with a truth to remember, a few questions to ponder, and a section called "Taking Action" where I suggest a project that will help you apply what you have read to your own life.

I am grateful to Len Goss of Broadman & Holman Publishers for his encouragement and wise insights. David and ClarLyn Morris loaned me their cottage so I could get away for a few days to write the first draft of this book. And I am especially thankful to my wife Marlene and to my three boys, Josh, Mark, and Nick, for giving me everything that makes life worth living.

No question is more basic than finding out what it means to be a real Christian. You may think you already know the answer, or maybe you're not sure. Either way, this is where we all need to begin. In order to discover the answer, let's step back two thousand years and listen in as Jesus has a nighttime conversation with Nicodemus. If you'd like to know what Jesus said to a very religious man, turn the page and let's get started.

Chapter 1

WHAT IS THE DIFFERENCE BETWEEN A REAL CHRISTIAN AND A RELIGIOUS PERSON?

Let's begin with a simple question. What percentage of people in America believe in God? You probably won't be surprised to know that the number is very high. One recent survey puts it at 94 percent.[1] That means that almost nineteen out of twenty people believe in God. It also means you won't run into very many atheists at the supermarket. Let's try a second question. What percentage of Americans call themselves Christian? That number is also high, but not as high as the number who believe in God. Approximately 83 percent of those surveyed claim to be Christian.[2]

A study of the poll results suggests something like this: Almost everyone believes in God and most people consider themselves Christian. It appears that for many people being a Christian is primarily a matter of birth ("I'm a fourth-generation Presbyterian.") or church affiliation ("I joined a Baptist church twenty years ago.") or perhaps even of citizenship ("I'm an American and this is a Christian nation, so I must be a Christian, right?"). When the question is asked, "Do you consider yourself to be 'born again' or 'evangelical'"? the percentage answering yes drops to 46 percent.[3] Evidently there is a big difference in the minds of many people between being a Christian and being "born again."

And that brings us to the question posed in the chapter title: What's the difference between a real Christian and a religious person? The question itself comes from an unsigned slip of paper turned in by someone in my congregation. Whoever wrote this question deserves an A+ for creativity and for getting right to the point. The wording suggests that there is a fundamental difference between being religious and being a "real Christian." Many people have trouble with that concept because they think that if you are religious, then you must be a "real Christian." If you asked such people, "Are you a Christian?" they would reply, "I'm a church member" or "I've been baptized" or "I go to Sunday school" or "I go to Mass every week." But those answers raise another important question: Is being a Christian simply a matter of outward activity?

At this point most of us would instinctively answer no because we've all known people who go through the religious motions and have signed on the dotted line, so to speak, but who don't act like true Christians ought to act. We all know religious people whose religion seems to be only skin deep. It doesn't touch the weightier matters of justice, kindness, compassion, grace, and practical holiness.

That leads me to a very personal question that I would like you to ponder as you read this chapter. Here it is: *Am I a real Christian or am I just a religious person?*

It's one thing to be religious; it's another thing to be a real Christian. As we think about this truth, I'd like to draw your attention to the story of a man who came to Jesus one night. I begin here because this is perhaps the clearest example of a religious person who discovered when he met Jesus that his religion wasn't enough to meet the need of his own heart.

Many people today are looking for supernatural reality. Solomon said in Ecclesiastes 3:11 that God has put eternity inside every heart. Man is incurably religious by nature. That's why every human society—no matter how primitive—has some concept of a higher power, some vision of a reality that goes beyond the natural. On one level that explains why science has not eradicated religion from the earth. Science can never do that because technological achievement can't meet the deepest needs of the human heart. That's why every morning millions of people read their horoscopes and millions more watch the Psychic Friends Network.

Several years ago a book purporting to find hidden messages in the Hebrew text of the Old Testament climbed to the top of the best-seller list. That would seem to be a rather esoteric subject for a best-seller, yet hundreds of thousands of copies were sold. People are hungry for spiritual truth. If they cannot find it by normal means, they will reach for anyone or anything that claims to give them an answer.

By the same token, many people seek deeper reality through organized religion. They join the church, are baptized, confirmed, give their money, attend services faithfully, pray daily, read the Bible, and in general obey the rules of the church, hoping that by their outward performance they can find inner peace and a deep relationship with the God who made them. But the most religious person eventually discovers that religion alone cannot satisfy. All that feverish activity cannot produce peace of mind or guarantee acceptance with God. In the end you will be looking to heaven and crying out, "Is that all there is?"

A Religious Man Who Needed God

With that we come to the story of Nicodemus and Jesus. Here is how John introduces us to this very religious man: "Now there was a man of the Pharisees named Nicodemus, a member of the Jewish ruling council. He came to Jesus at night and said, 'Rabbi, we know you are a teacher who has come from God. For no one could perform the miraculous signs you are doing if God were not with him'" (John 3:1–2).

In order to understand this story, we need to know two things about Nicodemus. First, he was a Pharisee. If you are a student of the Bible, you probably have a negative view of the Pharisees. You may think that all the Pharisees were legalistic hypocrites who hated Jesus. But that's not true at all. In the first century the Pharisees were widely respected for their intense piety and deep scholarship. They were men who devoted their lives to the study of the Torah and its application to daily life. They truly wanted to obey God's law. That meant studying the Bible for hours each day, praying two hours a day, giving a tithe of all they possessed, and in general, being scrupulously concerned about morality. There were only a few thousand Pharisees because not many men would make that kind of personal sacrifice. Those who did were held in high esteem.

Second, Nicodemus was a member of the Jewish ruling council. This was a select group of seventy men who served as a kind of combination Congress and Supreme Court. They adjudicated various disputes and settled legal matters so the Romans wouldn't have to get involved. As you might expect, only the leading men were elected to such a prestigious position. The fact that Nicodemus was part of the ruling council meant that he must have been highly respected by his peers. In twenty-first-century terms, he was like a United States senator or a Supreme Court justice.

That's the man who came to see Jesus one night in Jerusalem. But why come at night? Perhaps because he knew that Jesus was controversial and he couldn't risk being seen publicly. Or perhaps he wished to have time for a lengthy personal interview. I'm sure there were elements of curiosity mixed with a sense of duty. After all, this upstart rabbi known as Jesus had been gaining followers by the day. As a leader, Nicodemus had an obligation to find out more about this man.

Surely there is more to the story than that. The fact that he risked his own position to come to Jesus speaks of his own personal need. Note what he said: "I know you are come from God because no one can work these miracles you do unless God is with him." Nicodemus admitted that Jesus had been sent from God. He was no mere man; he was more than a teacher from Galilee. In Jesus, Nicodemus recognized the mark of divine parentage.

Being Religious Is Never Enough

All of this is meant to lead us to an important conclusion: *Being religious is never enough.* If it were, Nicodemus wouldn't have had the time or the interest to meet Jesus. But he came because despite all his religious activity there was still an aching void in his heart. Could it be that Jesus himself could fill that void?

That brings us to the answer Jesus gave to this cultured, educated, well-respected religious leader: "In reply Jesus declared, 'I tell you the truth, no one can see the kingdom of God unless he is born again.' 'How can a man be born when he is old?' Nicodemus asked. 'Surely he cannot enter a second time into his mother's womb to be born!' Jesus answered, 'I tell you the truth, no one can enter the kingdom of God unless he is born of water and the Spirit'" (John 3:3–5).

Let's focus on the key phrase "born again." In the original language it has a double meaning. The word can mean "again" or "above." In this case both meanings apply. Jesus told Nicodeumus that the only way to find what he was looking for was to be born again from above. Despite all his learning, Nicodemus was utterly baffled by this thought. Is it possible to reenter his mother's womb a second time? No, that's not what Jesus meant. He was not talking about a second physical birth, but about a second spiritual birth. You are born once physically. That physical birth introduces you to the physical world. But if you want to enter the kingdom of God (the world of spiritual reality), you need a spiritual birth.

Lest Nicodemus misunderstand this truth, Jesus added an important fact: "You should not be surprised at my saying, 'You must be born again'" (John 3:7). Notice the tense of that statement. You *must* be born again. The new birth is not optional for any of us. Jesus didn't say, "I recommend that you be born again" or "You should be born again if after investigation it seems to meet your personal need" or "I think it would be a good idea to be born again." No! Jesus used the urgent language of forceful command: You *must* be born again.

Before we go on, let me remind you that Jesus spoke these words not to some immoral outcast but to one of the most religious men of his day. By any human standard, Nicodemus was a very good man and certainly a man we would admire for his intense devotion to God. Yet Jesus told him, "You must be born again."

Have You Been Born Again?

If he needed to be born again, what about you and me? Let me put the question to you directly: Have you ever been born again? Just in case I haven't made myself clear, I'm not asking about your church membership, your baptism, your confirmation, your giving record, your Sunday school attendance, or your personal morality. Nicodemus had the religion part down cold, but Jesus said, "You must be born again."

I know it is easy to misunderstand what I am saying because being born again is big news. Recently the newspapers printed a story about a major NFL star who now says that he is born again. As I read the story, it sounded genuine to me, but I could not help noticing how the writers struggled to come to grips with the whole notion of the new birth. To some it sounds like a cop-out; to others, the final step before joining some weird suicide cult.

But as far as Jesus is concerned, there is nothing strange about it. All of us need to be born again.

- Good people need the new birth.
- Religious people need the new birth.
- Church members need the new birth.

We all need to be born again, and if we're going to go to heaven, we *must* be born again. Without it, none of us will ever see the kingdom of God.

As you read this chapter, I'd like you to slow down for a moment and ponder the next sentence because it could change your life. *Nicodemus represents all of us.* He stands for every good, decent, law-abiding, upstanding citizen who ever lived. He was a good man who knew about God, but he didn't know God personally. That's the enigma of his personality. His story reminds us that religion is good, but the new birth is essential.

We need what Nicodemus needed because we stand in exactly the same place. We need a vital experience of spiritual rebirth. In short, we need what Jesus talked about two thousand years ago.

You Must Do What Nicodemus Did

That brings me to the central issue. If you want what Nicodemus found, you must do what Nicodemus did.

1. *He admitted his need.* He did that by taking a personal inventory of his life and realizing that despite all his best efforts, something vital was missing on the inside. In summing up his virtues—which were many and genuine—this good man came to the conclusion that he needed "something else" in his life. He didn't know what it was; he couldn't put his finger on it. But deep within he sensed that his religion—sincere though it was—could not fill the gaping hole in his heart.

Nothing else matters until you come to the same conclusion about your life. As long as you go blithely on your merry way thinking that everything is OK with your life, you can never be born again. It simply cannot happen to you because you do not feel your need for God's intervention in your life. You must start in the same place that Nicodemus started—with a sense of your own desperate need of God.

2. *He came to Jesus personally.* By that I mean he came on his own, by himself, individually, man to man. He sought and found the Son of God. Nicodemus could never have sent someone in his place. Nor could a committee have met his need. Salvation involves a personal, individual commitment of your heart to Jesus Christ. No one can do it for you, and you can't make that commitment for anyone else.

3. *He trusted Christ completely.* I realize the text doesn't reveal to us the fact of his conversion, but I think it may be inferred. After the death of Jesus, Nicodemus helped Joseph of Arimathea take the dead body of Jesus Christ down from the cross (John 19:39). This means he had "crossed the line" and was now willing to identify with Jesus publicly. The most famous verse in the Bible—John 3:16—occurs in this passage and promises eternal life to those who "believe" in him— that is, in Jesus Christ. To believe means to rely on Christ so completely—to trust him so utterly and selflessly—that you are casting all that you are and all that you have and all that you hope to become on Jesus Christ as your Savior and Lord.

Nicodemus did this. So must you if you would be born again.

Four Steps to the New Birth

You may be saying at this point, "I'd like this kind of personal relationship with Christ, but I don't know where to begin or what I should do." Let me make it clear by sharing with you four steps that lead to the new birth. Two steps deal with God and two steps deal with man.

Step 1: God loves you and wants you to know him. The most famous verse in the Bible comes from Jesus' discussion with Nicodemus.

John 3:16 tells us that God offers "eternal life" to anyone who will believe in Jesus Christ. God makes the same offer to you that he makes to the entire world. He truly wants you to be forgiven and to spend eternity with him in heaven.

Step 2: Your problem is sin, which separates you from God. Romans 3:23 tells us that "all have sinned and fall short of the glory of God." That simply means that no one is perfect because all of us have sinned in thought, word, and deed. Do you know how many sins it takes to send you to hell? Just one—and most of us can take care of that first sin before we ever get out of bed in the morning.

Step 3: God's remedy for your sin is the cross of Christ. Romans 5:8 says that "God demonstrates his own love for us in this: While we were still sinners, Christ died for us." By his death on the cross, Jesus Christ took your place, died the death you should have died, and paid the penalty for all your sins.

Step 4: Your response is to trust Jesus Christ as Savior and Lord. Revelation 3:20 reminds us that Christ stands at the door of your heart knocking, knocking, knocking. Perhaps you've seen that famous painting of Christ standing outside a lovely English cottage. He's obviously come for a visit, but no one will let him in. Everything seems normal in the painting until you pause to look at the door. Something is missing. There is no doorknob! Why? Because the door to the heart is always locked from the inside. Christ is a perfect gentleman. He will not barge in where he is not wanted. He always waits for someone to open the door.

"That's Amazing!"

But how can we know if we are truly trusting Christ? What kind of faith is genuine saving faith? If you know what it means to believe a doctor when he says, "You need surgery," you know what it means to have faith. If you know what it means to step into an airplane entrusting your safety to the captain in the cockpit, you know what it means to have faith. If you know what it means to ask a lawyer to plead your case in court, you know what it means to have faith. Faith is total reliance upon another person to do that which you could never do for yourself.

How much faith does it take to go to heaven? It depends. The answer is not much and all you've got. If you are willing to trust Jesus Christ with as much faith as you happen to have, you can be saved. But if you're holding anything back, thinking that maybe you need to do something to help save yourself, forget it! True saving faith expresses itself by reaching out to take Christ as our Savior and Lord—and not before then.

- It may be expressed through a prayer of personal trust in Christ.
- It may be expressed through baptism.
- It may be expressed through a "public profession."

But those things alone are not saving faith. Saving faith understands the gospel, believes the gospel, and then commits to the gospel as the only hope of salvation. Saving faith reaches out and trusts Christ as Lord and Savior.

While serving as a guest host on a national radio program, I took a call from a young girl named Angela who asked how you can know you are saved. I quoted 1 John 5:13, which says that you can know you have eternal life through believing in Christ. I told Angela that salvation depends on trusting Jesus Christ. It's more than just believing facts about Jesus. To trust in Christ means to rely completely upon him. Trust is what you do when you fly in a plane. You trust the pilot to get you back down on the ground safely. You trust a doctor when you take the medicine he prescribes. You trust a lawyer when you let him represent you in court. God says that when you trust Jesus Christ in that same way you are saved from your sins. All you have to do is trust Christ completely and you can be saved. When I asked Angela what she thought about that, she blurted out, "Wow! That's amazing." Yes it is. It's the most amazing truth I know.

Let's review those four steps to the new birth.

1. Do you understand that God loves you and wants you to know him?
2. Do you admit you are a sinner and unable to save yourself?
3. Will you accept the death of Christ as the sufficient payment for all your sins?
4. Are you ready to open the door of your heart and invite Christ to come in?

"Take Me to the Cross"

It all comes back to the cross, doesn't it? In one of his sermons, Billy Graham tells of a little boy lost in one of the large cities of northern England. When a police officer found him, the little boy was weeping because he couldn't find his way. The officer began suggesting various streets, shops, and landmarks, hoping something would jog the boy's memory. But nothing worked. Finally the officer remembered that there was a church in the middle of the town with an illuminated cross that stood above the skyline. Pointing to the cross, he asked the lad, "Do you live anywhere near the cross?" Suddenly brightening, the boy cried out, "Sir, take me to the cross and I can find my home." Millions of people today need to come to the cross of Christ, and when they do, they will find their way home to God.[4]

Let's return one more time to the question I asked in the beginning: Are you a real Christian or just a religious person?

- A religious person goes through the routine but doesn't have the reality inside.
- A real Christian knows Jesus Christ because he or she has been born again.

Princess Diana

What is your relationship with Jesus Christ? Do you know him personally? Many wonder, "If I die, what will happen to me?" That's an important question because all of us will die sooner or later. Think for a moment about the terrible tragedy that befell Princess Diana in Paris. When she left the hotel that night, she had no idea that she would be dead before the morning. She never dreamed that she would soon stand before God. But death came suddenly and tragically. The same thing may happen to any of us at any moment. Who can be sure of lasting even one more day?

With all my heart I urge upon you the importance of a personal relationship with Jesus Christ. Here is the good news of the gospel in one sentence: Your life can be transformed through Jesus Christ!

- Some are trapped in bitterness.
- Some are trapped in addiction.
- Some are trapped in sinful habits.
- Some are trapped in deep personal confusion.

Some are like Nicodemus—very religious, very decent, very moral, very hardworking, very good by all the standards of goodness, and yet you wonder deep inside, "Is that all there is?" Jesus said, "You must be born again." That can happen to you even as you read these words. In a matter of moments your life can change forever.

What will happen if you are born again? First, your sins will be forgiven by God (Eph. 1:7). Second, you will be given a brand-new life—the abundant life Jesus talked about (John 10:10). Third, you will never face God's judgment—you will never go to hell (John 3:18). Fourth, you will be declared "not guilty" and "justified" in the eyes of God (Rom. 4:5). Fifth, you can know you are going to heaven when you die (1 John 5:13). All these things are given to you by God the moment you say "Yes" to Jesus Christ.

You must make a personal decision about Jesus Christ. No one can make it for you. Your parents may be godly people, but that doesn't make you a Christian. You may have many fine Christian friends, but they cannot believe in your place. When it comes to the new birth, no one can be born again on your behalf. You must come to Christ on your own and put your faith in him as Savior and Lord.

Would You Like to Be Born Again?

Would you like to be born again? It could happen right now. You can start over right now. Your life can change in this moment. Ponder the words of this little verse:

Upon a life I did not live,
Upon a death I did not die,
I risk my whole eternity.

That is what it means to be a Christian. It means trusting in Christ so much that you risk your eternity on what he did for you in his life and in his death. I have sometimes told people that trusting Jesus for salvation means to trust him so completely that if he can't take you to heaven, you aren't going to go there. Are you willing and ready to do that?

Perhaps it will help you to form your words into a very simple prayer. Even while I encourage you to pray this prayer, I caution you that saying words alone will not save you. Prayer doesn't save. Only Christ can save. But prayer can be a means of reaching out to the Lord in true saving faith. If you pray these words in faith, Christ will save you. You can be sure of that.

> Dear Lord Jesus, I know I am a sinner. I realize my sins have separated me from God. I believe that Jesus Christ is the Son of God. I believe he died on the cross for my sins. I believe he rose from the dead on the third day. Here and now, with all my heart, I trust Jesus Christ as my own Savior and Lord. Come

into my heart, Lord Jesus, and save me. Make me a
brand-new person and give me a brand-new life. In
Jesus' name, Amen.

If you have prayed this prayer in sincere faith, you may want to
put your initials by the prayer along with today's date as a reminder
that you have come to Christ in faith, trusting him as your Lord and
Savior. I also encourage you to tell someone else *today* that you have
trusted Jesus Christ as your Lord and Savior.

Let's return one final time to our original question: What's the
difference between a real Christian and a religious person? A religious
person has religion; a Christian has been born again through personal
faith in Jesus Christ. It's as simple as that. Religion is good, but Jesus
is better. And he's the one who said, "You must be born again."

A Truth to Remember:
Even the best of us need to be born again.

Going Deeper

1. Do you have to be religious in order to go to heaven? List several religious activities that people often substitute for personal saving faith in Jesus Christ.
2. Why can't our good works save us? If good works can't save us,
   then why be good at all? What is the value of our good works
   once we have come to know Christ as Savior and Lord?
3. Jesus said, "You must be born again." In your own words,
   define what it means to be "born again." Describe in a few
   words how you came to know God personally.
4. Why is Jesus' death on the cross so important for our salvation? What does it mean to say that Christ died "for our sins"?
5. According to 1 John 5:13, what is the one condition for
   receiving eternal life from God?

6. Explain what it means to trust Christ as Savior. What is the crucial difference between intellectual faith (mental assent to facts) and true saving faith?

Taking Action

This chapter asks, "What is the difference between a real Christian and a religious person?" In the space below, write a brief answer to that question.

Chapter 2

CAN I LOSE MY SALVATION?

This is a controversial question in Christian circles. It would be difficult to find a subject about which believers are more deeply divided. To the question, "Can I lose my salvation?" there are whole denominations that answer yes: the Methodists, the Wesleyans, the Pentecostals, the Church of Christ, and (in a different sense) the Roman Catholic Church. To varying degrees, and in varying ways, people in these churches argue that under some circumstances a genuine Christian may lose his salvation and be denied entrance into heaven.

On the other side are the Baptists, the Presbyterians, and all of the Reformed churches. They insist that a true believer may sin and sin terribly but that in the end all who are truly saved will finally enter heaven. This doctrine goes by several terms:

- eternal security,
- once saved, always saved, and
- perseverance of the saints.

Part of the problem people feel with this doctrine is the declaration that true Christians inevitably go to heaven. It's difficult for us who live in a very uncertain world to believe that anyone can be that certain of heaven. How can you be sure? Does this teaching not invite pride and even possible spiritual laziness? Is not this doctrine damnable (as some have suggested) because it encourages believers to sin since they have nothing to lose? These are fair questions that I will try to address in this chapter.

There are two main reasons why some people think you can lose your salvation. First, they point to certain Scripture passages that contain severe warnings of judgment to Christians. Second, they also point to professing Christians who fall away from their faith or turn from holiness to live in continued sin. If we are honest, we must admit that this is a serious problem in every congregation. All of us know cases of apparently born-again believers who either drifted away from the church or fell into outright sin. Some repent and return, but others do not. What shall we say about them? Have they lost their salvation? Did they ever have it in the first place?

The eternal security debate is of supreme importance because it leads directly to the whole question of Christian assurance. Can Christians know with certainty that they are going to heaven when they die? Let me make that more precise. Is it possible to be 100 percent certain, beyond the shadow of any doubt, that no matter what happens to you in the future, you are going to heaven when you die? If you can lose your salvation—even theoretically—then the answer must be no. You can hope for heaven, you can believe in heaven, you can do your best to get there, but in the end you can never be sure. Jack Wyrtzen, founder of the great Word of Life ministry, used to say, "I'm as sure of heaven as if I'd already been there ten thousand years." Can a Christian really say that? Or is it just wishful thinking?

Let me give you my own answer to the question, "Can I lose my salvation?" In my mind the answer is simple: *It depends on who saved you.*

- If God saved you, you can't lose it because it depends on God.
- If you saved yourself, you can lose it because it depends on you.

Your salvation is eternally secure if God did the saving. But if you think that salvation is a cooperative venture between yourself and God—where you do a part and he does a part—then you're in big trouble because anything you start, you could mess up somewhere along the way. But if God started it, he'll also finish it.

Five Pillars of Biblical Truth

I am sure there are many ways of dealing with this question. For our purposes I'd like to share with you five pillars of biblical truth that lead me to believe that those whom God saves he saves forever.

Pillar #1: Salvation Is of the Lord
(Jon. 2:9; Luke 3:6; Rev. 7:10)

This is the fundamental truth, the place where all our thinking must begin. When Jonah was in the belly of the great fish, he cried out, "Salvation comes from the LORD" (Jon. 2:9). Luke 3:6 speaks of "God's salvation" and Revelation 7:10 tells us that "salvation belongs to our God" and to the Lamb. What does this mean? It means that salvation is a divine work of God. It is that act by which he rescues from sin all those who trust Jesus Christ as Savior and Lord. All three persons of the holy Trinity combine to procure salvation: God ordained it, the Son purchased it, the Holy Spirit applies it. We are chosen by God, called by the Holy Spirit, and saved by the blood of Jesus Christ.

It is precisely at this point that we must think very clearly. Many Christians believe that, although salvation is of the Lord, they have a part to play as well. They seem to think that salvation is 99 percent of God and maybe one percent dependent on what they do. It is not so. Even the faith to believe comes as a gift from God (Eph. 2:8). Even the power to choose the Lord must come from the Holy Spirit. Let us unite in saying that our salvation is God's gracious gift that we receive through faith. It's not that God has done the hard part and we must do the easy part; it's that God has done every part and enabled us to receive what he has graciously given.

Pillar #2: What God Starts, He Finishes (Phil. 1:6; Rom. 8:29–30)

Philippians 1:6 assures us that the "good work" of salvation that God has begun in us will be completed until the day of Jesus Christ. When Paul says that he is "confident" of these things, he uses a very strong Greek word that really means "fully persuaded" or "absolutely certain." It means to have no doubt whatsoever about the outcome.

But this makes sense when you understand that salvation is God's work from start to finish. After all, all of us as humans leave some things undone in life. Just take a look in your closet or your drawer or your garage (or the files on your computer) and you will find ample evidence of unfinished business. We start our projects with great enthusiasm, only to lay them aside because of time pressure, conflicting commitments, financial difficulty, or other problems that confront us. Sometimes we come back and finish those projects later, but often years pass and the dreams of yesterday slowly fade into distant memories.

Not so with God. He finishes what he starts. When God determines to save a person, he saves him. Period. Consider the "golden chain" of salvation in Romans 8:29–30. Paul expresses the five links of the chain this way: foreknown, predestined, called, justified, glorified. The first two refer to God's decision to save those who trust in Christ; the second two terms refer to God's activity in actually saving those whom he has chosen. But the last phrase—"glorified"—refers to what happens when God's children finally get to heaven. When we stand before the Lord in resurrection bodies, free from sin forever, we will be in a glorified state.

But how is it that Paul can express this truth about our future glorification in the past tense? The answer is simple. Paul says it in the past tense because it is so certain of fulfillment that it is as if it had already happened. You might say that with God the work is already done. Since he lives outside space and time, the past, present, and future are all the same to him. While we're living on earth, from God's point of view we're already in heaven. From our point of view, that's impossible, but from God's standpoint our glorification in heaven is an accomplished fact. Thus we may be sure of our salvation because when God starts to save someone, he doesn't give up halfway through the process. He saves that person completely and eternally.

Pillar #3: Eternal Life Begins the Moment You Believe (John 3:36; 5:24; 6:37–40; 10:27–28)

Sometimes we use the term *eternal life* to refer only to that which happens to us after we die. We think this life and eternal life never overlap. But the biblical concept is quite different. In the Bible, "eternal life" is nothing more or less than the life of God himself. Because he is eternal, the life he gives is eternal. And that life begins the moment a person believes. According to Jesus' own words, a believer "has" eternal life as a present possession (John 3:36), he has "crossed over" from death to life (John 5:24), he cannot "perish" (John 3:16), he will never be driven away by Christ (John 6:37), Christ will lose none of those entrusted to his care (John 6:39), and no one in all creation will snatch a believer from the hand of Christ (John 10:28). It is hard to imagine how words could be any plainer to express the security of a true believer.

Think of it this way. If eternal life begins the moment you believe, and if it's truly eternal, then how can you lose it? If you lose it, it's not really eternal, but temporary. In that case, we should talk about "temporary life" instead of "eternal life."

Pillar #4: Justification Secures Our Eternal Pardon (Rom. 8:33)

The word *justify* means "to declare righteous." The term comes from the courtroom of the first century. As a trial drew to a close, the judge, having heard all the evidence, would pronounce his verdict. To justify a person meant to declare that he was not guilty in the eyes of the law.

There is another way to understand the term. If you have a computer, you probably know what it means to have justified margins. A "justified" margin is one that is absolutely straight from top to bottom. The computer arranges the words and spaces so that all the lines end up at exactly the same place. In that sense to justify means "to make straight that which would otherwise be crooked."

Now take those two concepts and put them together. When you trust Jesus Christ as Savior, God declares you "not guilty" of sin and "straight" instead of "crooked" in his eyes. It is an act entirely of God performed by God on the basis of Jesus' death on the cross and is received by us through the instrumentality of faith. Nothing you do and nothing you ever could do contributes to your own justification. It is entirely an act of God on the sinner's behalf. The crooked is declared to be straight and the guilty sinner is declared righteous in God's eyes.

Let's take that truth and apply it to Romans 8:33, "Who will bring any charge against those whom God has chosen? It is God who justifies." What if someone wants to accuse us before God? Can anyone bring a charge against us and make it stick? Satan comes and testifies against us in the court of heaven, "Get rid of him! He's a bum! He's a sinner! Did you see what he did? Did you hear what he said? Do you know where she went last night?" Who is there who can bring a charge that can stick in the ears of Almighty God? The answer is no one! Not even Satan. Why? Because it is God who justifies.

Who can bring a charge against the people of God? Shall the law bring a charge against us? No, because the law was fulfilled in Jesus Christ. Shall the devil bring any charge against us? He can try, but it won't work because he was defeated by the Lord Jesus Christ. Not anyone, not any angel, nor any demon, nor anyone in heaven or on earth or under the earth, or anybody we know could bring a charge against us in the ears of God. No one can say, "Oh God, you have chosen this person but she has disgraced you; you ought to get rid of her."

It is God who justifies. That means the judge of the universe is on our side. There is no one who can bring a charge against you who will ever cause your salvation to be in jeopardy. God will not listen to that charge. For the sake of his Son, the Lord Jesus Christ, he has justified you. When God justifies you, you stay justified. When God says "not guilty," nobody can ever condemn you nor can you ever be guilty again.

Pillar #5: Nothing Can Separate Us from the Love of Christ (Rom. 8:38–39)

This point comes from the magnificent closing verses of Romans 8 where Paul summons all creation to witness to the security of those whom God has called to salvation. The list would appear to be exhaustive:

Neither death nor life,

Neither angels nor demons,

Neither the present nor the future,

Nor any powers,

Neither height nor depth,

Nor anything else in all creation.

None of this—or all of this taken together—or any of it gathered in small parts—can separate the true believer from the love of God in Christ Jesus our Lord.

Someone may ask if it is possible for a believer to take himself out of God's grace. Upon first blush the answer would seem to be yes. You believed, so certainly you could "unbelieve" if you wanted to. And some people have apparently done that. They have recanted their Christianity and returned to their former beliefs or gone back into the world and followed the path of sinful excess.

Surely God would not continue to save such a person, would he? We can answer that in two ways.

First, in the great majority of such cases we may say with assurance that such persons were never true believers in the first place. Their faith was the profession of a religious person, not the saving faith the Bible talks about. They professed what they did not possess. Since they were never saved in the first place, they couldn't lose what they never had.

Second, in the remaining minority of cases we may simply reply that God saves whom he desires to save. There may well be some people in heaven who truly believed but later recanted but were saved as a demonstration of the depth of God's amazing grace. How can I say that? Because Romans 8:39 says that nothing in all creation can separate us from the love of God in Christ Jesus our Lord. We can't even separate ourselves from that saving love! Are you part of God's creation? If the answer is yes, then even you can't "unsave" yourself. This is surely the most stupendous truth relating to eternal security.

Remember, we are all saved in the end in spite of ourselves and not because of anything we do. That's why your salvation doesn't rest on you; if it did, you would never go to heaven. And neither would I.

I can summarize everything I have said so far in three simple statements:

1. God has done everything necessary to make you eternally secure.
2. Eternal security is the reason you can know you are going to heaven when you die.

3. That is why Romans 8:1 says there is "no condemnation" to those who are in Christ Jesus.

I conclude from all this that it is impossible for a truly regenerated person—that is, a born-again Christian, one who has experienced God's salvation—to ever lose his salvation. God has promised to save that person forever and to take him to heaven when he dies. And God always keeps his promises.

Four Categories of Problem Passages

Having presented the biblical truth regarding eternal security, it is important to balance it by considering the numerous problem passages often brought forward by those who believe you can lose your salvation. While I don't have time or space to comment on each passage individually, I think it's important to at least comment on the major categories. I find that the warning passages for the most part fall into one of four broad categories.

Passages Addressed to False Professors

Certain passages in the New Testament are warnings against false profession—that is, against religious activity without having Jesus in your heart. Such people might be very religious, but they are also very lost. Matthew 7:21–23 comes to mind as a primary example. There Jesus warns against people who work miracles in his name yet on the day of judgment he will say, "Depart from me. I never knew you." In all the New Testament, there is no better example of such a person than Judas. Although personally chosen by Christ and given the privilege of living with Christ for more than three years, he never committed himself to the Lord. As Acts 1:25 says, he went to "where he belongs" (that is, to hell) when he died because he was never a true believer in the first place. These warnings don't touch the question of losing your salvation because they are addressed to those who were never saved to begin with.

Warnings Regarding Losing Your Eternal Reward

Other passages often mentioned touch on the issue of a true believer losing his eternal rewards in heaven through unfaithfulness as a Christian. First Corinthians 3:15 speaks of "escaping through the flames" (not a reference to hell but to the blazing gaze of Jesus), and 1 Corinthians 9:24–27 speaks of Paul's buffeting of his own body lest he should become "disqualified"—that is, be removed from his ministry and lose God's blessing through sin. Second John 8 and 1 John 2:28 also refer to the same possibility. Again, none of these warnings deal with losing your eternal salvation, but rather with the real possibility of losing your eternal rewards in heaven.

The Danger of Facing Physical Judgment and Death

A third category of problem passages deals with the possibility of Christians facing physical sickness and imminent death because of sin. First Corinthians 11:30 speaks of believers who were sick, weak, and in some cases prematurely dead because of misbehavior at the Lord's Table. I would suggest that the "sin that leads to death" of 1 John 5:16–17, the exhortation to "save [a sinner] from death" in James 5:19–20, and the warnings of Hebrews 2, 6, 10, and 12 all fall into this general category. None of these passages warn against losing your salvation, but they do teach us that God takes seriously the sinful lifestyles of those who claim to be his children. When we get to heaven we will discover that some of us endured hardship, sickness, debilitating disease, and even premature death because of persistent unconfessed sin and willful disobedience to the Lord.

As Hebrews 12:4–11 teaches, God disciplines sinning believers. He "spanks" them—sometimes severely. Although we rarely hear about this today, the New Testament clearly warns that believers cannot sin with impunity.

Serious Calls to Holy Living

Finally, there are many passages that contain serious calls to holy living. Hebrews 12:14–15 says that without daily holiness no one will see the Lord. In one sense all believers are "holy" through our union with the holy Son of God, Jesus Christ. In another sense, holiness must be lived out on a daily basis as we seek the Lord in everything. When we do, we "see" the Lord—that is, we experience him in a deep and intimate way. When we choose to walk in the world, we miss that experience of God's presence. In the same vein, Ephesians 4:30 challenges us not to "grieve" the Holy Spirit through anger, malice, and other sins of the heart. When we do, we miss God's best for our lives.

Two Groups in View

Perhaps it would be good to offer some general comments on these various categories we have looked at briefly. First, not everyone is a Christian who claims to be a Christian. Second, how you live as a Christian matters to God. Third, there are present and future rewards for those who take their faith seriously. Fourth, there is present and future judgment for Christians who stray away from the Lord.

These problem passages basically have two groups in view:
Group 1: Those who are religious but not born again.
Group 2: True believers who fail to take their faith seriously.
Group 1 needs to be saved.
Group 2 needs revival, repentance, and restoration to God.
Group 1 needs to ask, "Am I truly born again?"
Group 2 needs to ask, "Am I walking with the Lord?"
Group 1 never had salvation.
Group 2 has taken it for granted.

But none of this touches the question of losing your salvation. The Bible never warns against losing your salvation because such a thing simply cannot happen.

A Roller-Coaster Christianity

The teaching that you can somehow lose your salvation carries with it several dangers. It may lead to excessive introspection, frustration, fear, and guilt. It strips you of any assurance of your salvation and may make you hypercritical of others whose faith you doubt. The Christian life can easily become an unstable roller coaster of up-and-down experiences. And worst of all, it takes the focus off Christ and places it on your own performance. In its extreme manifestation, it takes the "Good News" out of the gospel because you can't be sure about where you stand with God.

By the same token, there are great benefits to teaching eternal security. It puts the focus of salvation where it ought to be—on God and not on us. It also provides a basis for personal assurance and gives real hope in the moment of death. It also gives us proper motivation to pray for sinning believers. When eternal security is properly taught, it leads to a Christian life built upon love and gratitude—not doubt and fear. And it ought to produce a life of love, faith, and obedience to God. Finally, it points us toward heaven and to our eternal rewards.

A salvation you could lose is not much of a salvation at all. You can't be sure you have it, and if you have it today, you can't be sure you'll have it tomorrow. And if you lose it, you can't be sure you'll get it again. And if you get it again, you can't be sure you'll keep it the next time. What kind of salvation is that? It's a man-centered salvation that makes heaven dependent on what you do. Remember what I said earlier: it all depends on who saves you. If you save yourself, or if you think salvation is a cooperative venture between you and God, then you can certainly lose it. Anything you do for yourself, you can lose for yourself. But if God saves you, you are saved forever because it depends on him and not on you. What God does, he does forever.

Three Truths about Our Salvation

In stating the matter so plainly, I am keenly aware that not every evangelical would agree with what I have said. Some of the most godly Christians I have known believe that it is possible to lose your salvation. They walk with Christ, they serve him wholeheartedly, they share the Good News with others, and they have personal assurance of their own salvation. Most of them don't believe in the concept of being saved over and over and over again. They would agree that being saved over and over again produces a "roller-coaster Christianity."

Most of them believe in what I would call "soft" security. That is, they are convinced that as long as you continue to believe in Jesus, you are eternally secure. In their minds, the only way to lose that salvation is to totally and willfully reject Jesus Christ and his work on the cross—that is, to become an apostate. Short of that extreme step, you can rest assured of your salvation. I call that "soft" security because many people who believe that would actually agree with most of what I have said in this chapter. They simply hold out the *hypothetical possibility* that salvation could be lost through deliberate personal rejection of Christ.

I wish to say that I have wonderful fellowship with believers who differ with me on this point. In my mind, it all goes back to the fundamental question: Who saved you? If God saved you, your salvation rests on him. If you somehow contribute to the faith part of your salvation, then possibly their view is correct. But the Bible clearly teaches that even the faith to believe is a gift of God (Eph. 2:8). Therefore, I respectfully disagree with my dear friends and insist that salvation is forever, and is not dependent on our belief or even on our continuing belief but solely on the grace of God at work in us.

I should add one final point. Is it really possible for a truly saved person to literally and actually give up his faith entirely? If Hebrews 6:4–6 and Hebrews 10:26–31 are describing born-again people, then the answer is yes. Such individuals have put themselves beyond all human help. They have "crossed the line" and cannot be renewed to repentance. Thus, they face judgment as they fall into the hands of a living God for severe judgment and the possibility of imminent physical death.

It is also possible that these verses describe individuals who were never truly born again in the first place. Such people have truly hardened their hearts against the God they claimed to know intimately. Because God will not be mocked, there is nothing left for them but judgment. Perhaps we are left with the practical reality that "only God knows for sure" in such cases. In any case, I do not believe that Hebrews 6 and 10 describe losing your salvation.

Surprised by the Grace of God

Here are three concluding truths to ponder:

1. Since salvation begins and ends with God, we are as secure as he is.
2. Since God cannot lie, we can trust him to save us eternally.
3. Since heaven will be so wonderful, we'll never regret serving the Lord in this life.

There will be three surprises when we get to heaven. First, we're going to be surprised that some people are there that we didn't expect to see there. Second, we're going to be surprised that some people aren't there that we were sure were going to be there. Third, the greatest surprise of all will be that we ourselves are there.

We will be surprised by the grace of God! Heaven will be so much greater than we had imagined, and Christ himself so wonderful, that we will marvel that God would save people like us. The grace of God—which seems so great now—will seem much greater then. When we finally get to heaven, we will appreciate our salvation much more than we do now. In heaven we will see clearly why salvation is by God and

God alone. Between now and then, we can rest in a salvation that depends on God and not on us and is therefore eternally secure.

A Truth to Remember:

God has done everything necessary to make you eternally secure.

Going Deeper

1. Why is it important to understand that "salvation is of the Lord"? Do you agree that even the faith to believe in Christ is a gift of God?
2. Do you agree with the author that eternal security is a crucial doctrine for Christians to believe? Why or why not?
3. List three common objections to the doctrine of eternal security. How would you answer them? What important truths can be learned from studying those objections?
4. Do you agree with the author that when properly understood, this doctrine should promote holy living and deep gratitude to God? Why or why not?
5. Take a concordance and trace the words *justify* and *justification* through the New Testament. In simple terms, what does it mean to be justified? Why is this doctrine crucial to our understanding of eternal security?
6. In what way is salvation wrapped up in the character of God? What does it mean to say that "our salvation is as secure as he is"?

Taking Action

For seventeen years Sally was a loyal member of the Willow Bend Community Church. The two of you served together in a number of church organizations and committees. Ten months ago she abruptly resigned from all her duties and left the church. So far your efforts to talk to her have been politely rebuffed. She isn't going to church anywhere and shows no spiritual interest. "I don't know what I believe anymore," she says. No one seems to understand what has happened in her life. Has she lost her salvation? Was she never really saved? Is she a believer out of fellowship with the Lord? How can you help her? Based on this chapter, how should you be praying for her? How might your view of eternal security impact the way you answer these questions?

Chapter 3

WHICH CHURCH SHOULD I JOIN?

I live in a suburb of Chicago called Oak Park. Approximately fifty-three thousand people live here. On many street corners you can find a massive church structure. At the turn of the century, when Oak Park was the first affluent suburb on the railroad west from Chicago, the men driving the delivery wagons said it was easy to know when you entered Oak Park: "It's where the saloons end and the steeples begin." When the drivers coined that phrase, they were saying that Oak Park was a community filled with churches. A century later that observation is still true. Today there are sixty different churches representing more than twenty denominations.

What is true of Oak Park is true of many communities. Across America there are four hundred major denominations. There are over thirty different kinds of Baptists, more than a dozen varieties of Methodists, not to mention a large handful of Presbyterian and Lutheran churches. We can add to that the many Charismatic and Pentecostal churches and the large number of independent and inter-denominational churches. Although we often sing, "We are not divided, all one body we," the many divisions within Christendom show that we don't always mean it.

Look in the Yellow Pages under "Churches" and you are likely to discover a bewildering array of choices. How do you know which church you should join? For some people the answer is easy. They were raised Catholic or Baptist or Mennonite or Church of Christ and that's the end of the discussion. Others opt for whichever church is closest and has the most convenient schedule of services. Many parents don't mind which church they attend as long as their children are well cared for. And a growing number like to church shop, spending a few weeks here, a few weeks there, sometimes settling down, sometimes always moving on.

I should freely admit that I can't answer this question for you. I can't even tell you which denomination you should prefer above all the others. Churches are different, people are different, cultures are different, and family needs are different. What fits one person and one family may not fit another. So if you're looking for an answer along the lines of "Find the nearest Baptist/Lutheran/Episcopal/Assembly of God church and join it," you might as well skip this chapter altogether. I can't help you if that's what you need to know.

But I am sure of this much: You need a place to belong. To borrow a phrase from a famous television show, we all need a place where everyone knows our name. And we need a place where we can know and be known, where we can find some friends who will help us on our spiritual journey. In short, we need to be part of the family of God that is called the church. And not just the "church universal" that stretches around the world. We desperately need to put down some roots in a specific local church.

We should not be surprised at that since we've known for a long time that God made us as social creatures. No one is an island; no one is made to live entirely alone. We were made for friendship, for family, for deep, caring relationships. And when we don't find those, we search high and low until we do.

Deep in the Heart of Texas

It is said that home is where, when you go there, they have to take you in. A year ago my wife and I went "home" to Midlothian, Texas, a town about thirty miles south of Dallas. During my seminary days I served as assistant pastor of a church in Midlothian. In the two decades since our last visit, the church has more than tripled in size and moved to a new location. I wondered if anyone would remember us. But all fears were removed when we entered the beautiful new building and were immediately overwhelmed with hugs. We were nearly hugged to death. The people who knew us a quarter-century ago couldn't have been nicer.

As I reflected on it later, it occurred to me that almost no one asked what we had been doing for the last twenty years. They didn't ask how many books I had written or the size of the church I now pastor. That didn't seem to matter. And no one asked about the mistakes I've made over the years. How refreshing to be with people and not feel you have to pull out your résumé to prove your worth. That to me is what the body of Christ is supposed to be.

We find a similar truth in the New Testament. Acts 2:41–47 offers us a brief snapshot of the early church. In fact, this is the very earliest picture of what Christianity looked like in the beginning. I am impressed by the first and last verses of this passage. Verse 41 tells us the church began with three thousand conversions in one day. Can you imagine a church membership seminar for three thousand people? Verse 47 says that people were being saved daily and added to the church. The verses in between describe what happens when God breaks loose in a group of ordinary men and women. This is not religion or ritual but the reality of Christ at work in the midst of his people.

Five Marks of a Healthy Church

What sort of church should you join? This passage paints a picture of a vibrant, growing community of Christian believers. This is what Christianity looked like when it was a movement and not a world religion. From these verses we can discover five marks of a healthy church. Find a church with these five characteristics and you've found a good church to join.

Mark #1: Solid Grounding in the Word of God

Luke reports that the early believers devoted themselves to the "apostles' teaching" (Acts 2:42). This means they put a high priority on knowing the truth. Sometimes you see churches with names like "Apostolic Church of God in Jesus' Name #3," and you wonder, "What makes a church apostolic?" I answer that a church is apostolic if it follows the teaching of the apostles found in the New Testament. To the extent that any church follows the New Testament, that church is an apostolic church. This means that the Word of God must be the objective foundation of the church. A healthy church does not depend on the latest Gallup Poll or the whims of public opinion to decide what to believe or what to do. God still guides his church today through his inerrant, inspired, totally truthful Word.

Because the Bible is the Word of God, the people of God must consult it whenever they face a difficult decision. When thinking about the future of the church, the leaders must ask, "What does God say about this?" The same is true for all the members of the congregation. Christians must seek to know what God has said in his Word and then prayerfully apply it to their own situations.

Let me illustrate. Each year in January, churches across America observe Sanctity of Human Life Sunday. Christians from many denominations pause to reaffirm our conviction that all human life is sacred in the eyes of God and deserving of our protection. We especially wish to say we oppose legalized abortion and pray for God to lift this scourge from our land. Where does that conviction come from? Certainly not from our politicians. We came to that truth by simply reading the Bible and discovering what God says about unborn human life (see Ps. 139:13–16).

Ditto for homosexuality, adultery, political corruption, illegal drug use, and a host of other contemporary vices that grip our nation. Churches that believe the Bible aren't confused about any of those things because they can read the Bible. They don't appoint task forces to decide what they believe about abortion. They simply stand on God's Word without regard to whether or not this makes them popular with the powers-that-be.

Not long ago one of our local newspapers commented that some churches in Oak Park don't wish to be called "progressive." I thought to myself, *Thank God. That's the best news I've heard in years.* We need churches that are progressive in method but biblical in theology. Sometimes it is said that the church is twenty years behind the times. What a terrible insult. We ought to be two thousand years behind the times. If we can do that, we'll discover the same power that animated the early church.

During my sermon one Sunday a couple got up and walked out of the sanctuary, evidently upset by what I had said. One of our members had spoken to this couple before the service and learned that they were visiting a number of churches in our area. My friend commented that it is frightening in a way because it reminds us that the message of God's truth cuts both ways—it is "life" for some and "death" for others.

As the old hymn says, "How firm a foundation, ye saints of the Lord, Is laid for your faith in His excellent Word! What more can He say than to you He hath said, To you who for refuge to Jesus have fled?" God's Word is the all-sufficient foundation for every Christian and for every local church. If this be true, then each person should ask this question: Am I learning more about what God says and how to apply it to my life?

Mark #2: Vital, Life-Transforming Worship

Vital worship played an important role in the early church. Luke makes this clear in two ways. Verses 42 and 46 of Acts 2 mention "breaking of bread"—probably a reference to a meal followed by the Lord's Supper. Verse 47 adds that they were "praising God." The whole passage suggests a sustained atmosphere of praise and worship that permeated the early church. They didn't have just one stated "worship service" but evidently gathered daily to sing, praise, and share the Lord's Supper together.

One gets the sense that this was very active worship. During a recent concert, contemporary Christian musician Babbie Mason commented that the people in her home church understood that worship is a verb. She meant that the preacher always knows how he is doing because the people in the pews talk back to the speaker. They listen and say "amen" or offer other comments on the sermon. And when they sing, the congregation throws heart, soul, and body into the effort. The result is a transforming experience where every part of the worshiper is involved in praising God.

When the Bible describes worship, it mentions things like singing, clapping, shouting, laughing, kneeling, saying "amen," speaking, sitting in silence, chanting, praying, lifting up the hands, lying prostrate on the floor, beating the chest, crying, blessing God and others, joining hands, singing in the choir, listening to the choir, playing cymbals, horns, bells, pipes, trumpets, and even dancing. That tells us that worship is to involve the whole person in every area of life.

This is not an issue of style. After all, the worship of Acts 2 was synagogue worship brought over into the early church. If we were somehow transported back in time, we would not understand their songs or the Scripture reading or the sermon. Yet God blessed their worship and infused it with his Holy Spirit.

In my years of traveling I have raised my hands in charismatic worship in Belize, and I have worshiped in a tiny Russian church not far from the Volga River. Although the only words of Russian I knew were "good morning" and "yes" and "no," when the believers stood to sing the Lord's Prayer, I stood and sang along with them. During my last tour of the Holy Land, our group spent one Sunday night at the King of Kings congregation that meets in the Jerusalem YMCA. Many of the choruses were in Hebrew, yet we joined right in and worshiped God with our brothers and sisters. The same thing happened during an evangelistic crusade in Pignon, Haiti. When those dear brothers and sisters sang "Great Is Thy Faithfulness" in Creole, we sang along in English.

Recently I worshiped in several Nigerian churches. Sometimes we all sang in English and sometimes they sang hymns in Hausa and I sang along in English. I have sung "Just As I Am" with forty-five thousand others at a Billy Graham Crusade in Denver; listened with awe to the magnificent sound of "Holy, Holy, Holy" on a pipe organ; stood around a campfire in Schroon Lake, New York, with three hundred teenagers singing "We Are Climbing Jacob's Ladder"; heard the beautiful chanting of the Catholic monks at the Church of the Holy Sepulchre in Jerusalem; and attended an Orthodox liturgy in St. Petersburg, Russia. On a trip to Paraguay, my wife and I learned to sing *Hay Vida* in Spanish and one or two songs in the Guarani language. I have been in churches where the music was fast, slow, and in between; in formal liturgies and informal sharing services; in churches which followed the church year, and in churches where they never heard of the church year.

The test of true worship is that it should lift us into God's presence. Here is a simple test for worship: Does it whet your appetite for God? Biblical worship lifts you out of your own world and creates in your heart a hunger to know God better. In some ways style is almost irrelevant as long as people come into contact with the living God.

Mark #3: Caring Relationships with Other Believers

Acts 2:42 tells us that the first believers were devoted to "fellow-ship." The Greek word means "to share something in common." The rest of the passage fleshes out this concept as we learn that they were "all together" (v. 44), they met together in the temple courts (v. 46), and they ate together (v. 46).

This passage mentions three times that the people ate together. Shared meals played an important part in the life of the early church. Eating together is one mark of a united church. Sometimes ministers like to joke that if you want to get a group out, you have to have pie and coffee. If you want to get a crowd, you have to have a meal or at least you need refreshments. Sometimes people grumble about it. But it's not just a psychological fact that people like to eat together. It is also a biblical truth. In the earliest days of the church, Christians ate together every day. I believe the church that eats together will stay together, will play together, will pray together, will grow together in every sense of the word. I call this the *First Rule of Church Growth:* "If you feed them, they will come." Thousands of Wednesday night suppers have proved it to be true.

The early believers were all together all the time. That reminds me of Dr. W. A. Criswell's statement that the church should be the social center of the congregation. Thirty years ago that was a radical concept, but "Dr. C" was a man ahead of his time. Today the largest churches in America do the same thing—and attract great crowds of people. Not long ago I happened to see a banner hanging from a local church proclaiming something about their plans for the twenty-first century. Underneath were these words: "St. Giles Community of Faith." I like that concept—the church as a "community of faith." That's entirely in keeping with the spirit of Acts 2:41–47.

This idea of togetherness is so important because we live in increasing isolation from one another. Our technology has made it easier than ever to avoid human contact. Look at the average family. We have our own cars, our own rooms, our own phones, computers, beepers, pagers, and even our own fax machines. We can work at home if we want, thus avoiding the messy problem of dealing with people face to face. Our quest for more privacy has come at the cost of enormous personal loneliness.

There is nothing more important that I can say to you than this statement: *God never intended that you should live the Christian life by yourself.* He intended that the Christian life would not be a solo, but a duet, a trio, a quartet, a quintet, a choir, and a mighty symphony. He intended that as you joined your life with other people, they would help you and you would help them. How is it with you? Do you have a few people in your life who really know you? Or do you always wear the mask, the costume, play the game, because the show must go on? Are you accountable to anybody for the way you live? Or are you doing it all by yourself?

You may be struggling right now because you don't have a group, you're not close to anyone, and you're not accountable to anybody. God never intended that his children would live like hermits. He intended that they would live together, and that in living together, they would help one another along the way. It is God's will that we live together as brothers and sisters in a family relationship so that we can love one another, encourage one another, admonish one another, hug one another, pick one another up when we fall down, rejoice together, weep together, and correct one another when we make mistakes.

Here is the question to ask as you look for the right church: Does this church help me build relationships that encourage my spiritual growth? God never intended that you go it alone. A healthy church provides many opportunities to develop lasting personal relationships with other believers.

Mark #4: Seeing the Power of God through Prayer

The final item of verse 42 is "prayer." The early church was devoted to prayer. But don't skip past the next verse because there may be an important connection. "Everyone was filled with awe, and many wonders and miraculous signs were done by the apostles" (Acts 2:43). I think those three things should go together: *prayer . . . awe . . . wonders and signs.* Is it possible that miracles happened precisely because the believers prayed so fervently that an atmosphere of awe made such things possible? Matthew tells us that Jesus was not able to work many miracles in some cities because of their unbelief (Matt. 13:58). Could such a thing be true today? I know it's possible to go off on a tangent about "signs and wonders," but I also think it's possible to go off on a tangent in an unbelieving direction as well.

A friend called recently with news that he had visited the Brooklyn Tabernacle, a church with a dynamic ministry in a very challenging urban setting. Each week the church ministers to between eight and ten thousand people. They have excellent Bible teaching, great music, and warm fellowship. My friend reported that the Tuesday night prayer meeting draws the largest crowd each week. No wonder the church is growing.

Some years ago during a visit to a mission station in Belize, God impressed on my heart that if the church I pastored was going to the next level, we would get there only through prayer. The Lord clearly said that we wouldn't get there by preaching, programs, or publicity. Prayer must be the key. That seems elementary, doesn't it? What pastor wouldn't say that and what church doesn't believe it? Let me therefore repeat it once again—prayer is the key. It is not simply one of the keys. It is *the* key. Acts 2:42 tells us that the early disciples "devoted themselves . . . to prayer." Is it any wonder that as a result God gave them unity, miracles, and hundreds of people coming to Christ? All things are possible when a church prays.

I will leave you to ponder the matter yourself. Just before Jesus cleansed the temple, he declared, "My house will be called a house of prayer for all nations" (Mark 11:17). Christ intended that his people would pray and that as they prayed, they would pray for the nations, and people from all the nations would come and pray with them. It is no exaggeration to say that the Christian church was conceived in a prayer meeting (see Acts 1:12–14).

A great church devotes itself to prayer. And while a church may be large and active without prayer, it cannot be truly great without prayer. The question is very simple: Am I experiencing God's power in my life in answer to my prayers?

Mark #5: Practical Ways to Minister to Others

The final mark of a healthy church comes from Acts 2:44–45: "All the believers were together and had everything in common. Selling their possessions and goods, they gave to anyone as he had need." Some writers have suggested this was an early form of communism. That's misleading because communism was a malevolent twentieth-century ideology that enslaved millions of people. However, these verses do suggest a "commune-ism" of sorts in the early church. Evidently the believers lived together—or perhaps in close proximity to one another. Certainly they combined their resources to meet the needs of the poor in their midst.

I find it most interesting that as far as we can tell, no one told them to do this. They evidently did it on their own. Such a concept seems foreign to modern Christians—especially those in the West who value their personal possessions as part of their birthright. Why give up your hard-earned dollars for the sake of the poor? In Acts 2 the answer is simple: They valued people over possessions. They must have taken Jesus seriously when he spoke about not laying up treasures on the earth. This teaching is very threatening to many people today, so it is easier to find a way around it than to deal with it. While

I agree with those who say that we are not commanded to do exactly as they did, I also think we shouldn't ignore their example either.[5]

There is nothing in us by nature that would cause us to do what the early church did. So why did they do it? Recall for a moment the time when a rich young man visited our Lord and asked what he must do to inherit eternal life (Matt. 19:16–29). Jesus replied that he should keep the commandments. Being a serious young man, he asked, "Which ones?" Jesus listed several and included the commandment to love your neighbor as yourself. The young man felt good about it because he had kept all those commandments from his youth. Is there anything else? Here is the answer Jesus gave in Matthew 19:21: "If you want to be perfect, go, sell your possessions and give to the poor, and you will have treasure in heaven. Then come, follow me." Every time I read this passage, it seems like we have the right question (What must I do to inherit eternal life?) and the wrong answer. I doubt that any of us has ever given the answer Jesus gave to this young man. If you ask me how to inherit eternal life, I'll say something about accepting Christ as Savior. I may quote John 3:16 or Romans 5:8. But I won't quote Matthew 19:21.

Look at the five verbs in this verse: *go . . . sell . . . give . . . come . . . follow.* We're quite happy with the last two and not at all sure what to do about the first three. We're not comfortable with connecting following Jesus with selling all our worldly goods and giving the money to the poor. It seems a little radical.[6]

Luke 12:32 contains a wonderful promise: "Do not be afraid, little flock, for your Father has been pleased to give you the kingdom." Among other things, this is a promise that God has committed himself to provide for all our needs all the time. As citizens of the kingdom, we can rely on our Father to put all of heaven at our disposal. Before you start celebrating too much, let's read the next verse, "Sell your possessions and give to the poor" (Luke 12:33). Ouch! There it is again—sell what you have and give your money to the poor.

What does all this mean? I suggest that Jesus is teaching us that there is an intimate connection between our possessions, the way we treat other people, and our relationship with God. That's not a comfortable thought for many people because we prefer a compartmentalized faith where we can have our possessions, not worry about anyone else, and still be in good standing with the Lord. Jesus seems to be saying that it doesn't work that way. I mention Matthew 19 and Luke 12 because I think those passages help us understand Acts 2. Evidently the early Christians took the words of Jesus seriously and literally. That's why they did what they did. So the question is this: *Am I learning how to use my gifts to help others in a practical way?* Healthy churches make it easy for their members to be generous.

An Attractive Church without the "Stuff"

So what sort of church should you join? Should it be Baptist, Methodist, Presbyterian, Lutheran, Assembly of God, or should you join an interdenominational church? I can't answer that question for you, but I can say this. Find a church that looks a lot like Acts 2:41–47 and you've found a good church to join. As I stand back and look at the text, I see an attractive church. Here is a church with no building, no paid staff, no programs, no choir, no organ, no parking lots, no buses, no contemporary worship, and most amazingly, no Internet Web site. And yet they seemed to get along pretty well. In verse 41 we learn that three thousand people joined the church in one day; verse 47 adds that people were being saved by the Lord and added to their number daily. That's not bad, is it? Wouldn't you like to be part of a church like that?

They had none of the "stuff" most of us consider so crucial—yet they reached people by the thousands. I'm not arguing that the "stuff" is bad, only that their "stuff" (the five points I mentioned) is better than our "stuff." Ours is external; theirs touches the realm of the spirit. When I visited Nigeria, I never saw a church with the "stuff" an average American church has, yet I saw many churches with faith and zeal that were reaching people for Christ. Perhaps this explains why the church is growing fastest in so-called "Third World" countries where they aren't encumbered by the "stuff" we have. (I'm not arguing that these external items aren't useful for the gospel. They are, but they don't constitute the heart of a great church.)

What made the early church so attractive? It comes down to one thing and one thing only: They shared a common faith in Jesus Christ. On the Day of Pentecost, people gathered in Jerusalem from all points of the compass: Rome, Egypt, Crete, Cappadocia, Arabia, and many other places (Acts 2:1–11). That means the early church sprang from a "mixed multitude" of differing ethnic groups, skin colors, cultures, and languages. Their shared faith in Christ drew people to them.

Here are three key words that reveal the secret of the early church: *unified . . . magnified . . . multiplied.* The believers were *unified,* Christ was *magnified,* and the church was *multiplied.* The world has nothing like that. It can counterfeit that reality, but it can't duplicate it.

What are the marks of a healthy church? Here is the answer from Acts 2:41–47:

- founded on the Word of God,
- practicing vital worship,
- promoting caring relationships,
- devoted to prayer, and
- ministering to those in need.

Where those things are present, these five results are sure to follow:

- healthy on the inside,
- attractive on the outside,
- filled with joy,

- continual conversions, and the
- presence of God everywhere.

Find a church where these things are happening and you've found the right church. What happened in Acts 2 is not unique. It is possible whenever the church is the body of Christ and not simply an institution. This is God's plan. It still works today.

A Truth to Remember:

We all need a place where we can experience the reality of Christ with other believers who can help us in our spiritual journey.

Going Deeper

1. Name several different ways the word *church* is used today. Approximately how many churches are in your own community? Why is it crucial that Christians be part of a local church?

2. A healthy church believes the Bible. Yet even among evangelical churches, there are many points of disagreement. What doctrines are essential and thus nonnegotiable for a local congregation? What happens when these doctrines are neglected or even denied?

3. Why are musical styles often controversial in many churches today? What principles should guide our discussions in this area?

4. One writer says that people choose a church with their noses: "They can smell the joy." What does that statement mean? Do you agree?

5. What are the signs that a local congregation is truly "devoted to prayer"?

6. Name some of the outward, visible "stuff" that we consider essential for a successful church today. How many of those things were not available in the first century? How did the early believers succeed without them?

Taking Action

You've just been appointed to a church planting task force at Spruce Pine Baptist Church. Your pastor has a vision for starting a congregation in a bustling new development on the west side of town. At the first meeting the chairman asks, "What should the new church look like?" And he wasn't talking about the building. At the next meeting each member of the task force will be asked to share their vision for the new church. When your time comes to speak, what will you say? What will your "ideal church" look like?

Chapter 4

WHAT DOES IT MEAN TO BE FILLED WITH THE SPIRIT?

This is the age of the Holy Spirit." So says one prominent church growth expert. He is not alone in this optimistic assessment. Many leaders would agree that there is more interest in the Holy Spirit today than at any other time in the last two thousand years. There are many reasons for this conclusion, but the greatest has to do with the rise of Pentecostal and Charismatic churches. It is no secret that many of the fastest-growing churches in the world are Pentecostal and Charismatic to one degree or another. It is, therefore, no surprise that more has been written on the person and work of the Holy Spirit in the last century than in the previous nineteen hundred years. One hundred years ago it was hard to find a book on the Holy Spirit. But times have changed. Every Christian bookstore carries several dozen titles relating to the Holy Spirit and his work in the world today. If you will pardon the image, the Holy Spirit has come out of the shadows and taken center stage in Christian theology.

Questions, Questions, Questions

There are many questions Christians ask about the Holy Spirit. Some are very basic, such as, Who is the Holy Spirit and how can he help me? Others are more controversial: What is the baptism of the Holy Spirit? Should all Christians speak in tongues? What is holy laughter?

In this chapter we want to focus on something very practical and personal: What does it mean to be filled with the Spirit? I believe this is one of the most important principles of the spiritual life. Learn this and you will discover a source of supernatural power that can help you every single day. As far as possible, I would like to set all controversy aside and impress upon your heart your great need to be filled with the Spirit. This is our great need. Indeed, this is the need of the hour—for God's people to discover what it means to be filled with the Spirit.

Some questions immediately rise to the surface: What does it mean to be filled with the Spirit? What difference does it make? How does it happen? But preeminent above all others is this question: Am I filled with the Spirit? What a question! What is your answer? Suppose someone asked, "Are you filled with the Spirit?" What would you say? It's not easy to answer and therefore makes us uneasy as we think about it.

Three Common Misconceptions

Before you can accurately answer a question like that, we need to know what the filling of the Spirit is—and what it isn't. Let me mention three common misconceptions.

1. It Is an Emotional Experience

This is probably the first thing that comes to mind for many of us. We hear of strange things happening in revival meetings. People begin to shake, tremble, fall on the floor, bark like a dog, laugh uncontrollably. Some weep, others shout, still others speak in strange tongues. All of this is done in the name of the Holy Spirit, and so many people assume that's what the filling of the Spirit is all about.

Without stopping to pass judgment, let me say clearly that the filling of the Spirit is not primarily an emotional experience. Those things I mentioned are not necessarily the mark of the Spirit's work in a person's life. This is not to say that some of those things might not be genuine. They might be, but what the Bible means by the "filling of the Spirit" is not primarily an emotional experience.

2. It Is Reserved for Special Christians

The second misconception flows from the first. Because we hear of these unusual things happening, and because they don't happen to every Christian, it's easy to think that the filling of the Holy Spirit is reserved for some special class of super-Christians. It's not true. The Bible clearly commands every Christian to "be filled with the Spirit."

3. It Is Controversial and Therefore Better Off Ignored

Again, this follows from the previous two misconceptions. Some people overreact to the excesses of others and dismiss the doctrine of the Spirit's filling. Some even refuse to discuss the entire doctrine of the Spirit. That's a huge mistake because the Holy Spirit is the One who brings the presence of Christ to our lives. Without going into controversy, may I simply say again that we desperately need the Holy Spirit today.

I remember some years ago hearing Dr. J. Vernon McGee give a commencement address at Dallas Theological Seminary. He was then in his eighties and near the end of a long and fruitful ministry. I've forgotten almost everything else he said that night, but one comment has stayed with me. He said that if he were starting his ministry over again, he would give much more attention to the person and work of the Holy Spirit. He would preach on the Spirit more frequently and attempt to lead people to depend on his power every day. Charles Haddon Spurgeon, the greatest preacher of the nineteenth century, said, "The grand thing the church wants in this time is God's Holy Spirit." More than anything else, we need to rediscover the Holy Spirit and learn anew to depend on him.

The Crucial Text: Ephesians 5:18

With that, we turn to the key text on this topic: Ephesians 5:18. Let me give it to you in several different translations: "Do not get drunk on wine, which leads to debauchery. Instead, be filled with the Spirit" (NIV). The New Living Translation gives a slightly different wording: "Don't be drunk with wine, because that will ruin your life. Instead, let the Holy Spirit fill and control you." Finally, we have this paraphrase by Eugene Peterson in *The Message:* "Don't drink too much wine. That cheapens your life. Drink the Spirit of God, huge draughts of him." I especially like the phrase: "Drink the Spirit of God." That's very picturesque, isn't it?

In order that we might have the teaching clearly in front of us, here are four observations from the text.

1. Note the Contrast between Wine and the Spirit

This is the most basic point of the verse. There is a direct parallel drawn between being drunk with wine and being filled with the Spirit. What precisely is the point of comparison between wine and the Holy Spirit? Doubtless, the issue is influence or control. A person under the influence of wine experiences altered behavior. He or she may say or do things he would not ordinarily do. Emotions may be heightened for a brief period, causing the person to experience anger followed quickly by elation followed quickly by depression. If the person drinks enough wine, the mental processes will be affected and one's decision-making ability will be radically altered—almost always with a negative result.

Likewise, the filling of the Holy Spirit produces a change in behavior. In the Book of Acts, once-timid disciples became flaming evangelists for Jesus Christ. In Ephesians 5:19–21 Paul mentions three practical results of the filling of the Spirit: singing, a thankful heart, and an attitude of mutual submission. The last result is most significant because true submission always involves giving up your right to be in control in every situation. When we submit from the heart, we are saying, "I don't have to have my way all the time." Only a heart touched by the Holy Spirit can maintain such an attitude in every relationship of life.

2. This Is a Command

In the Greek language this verb is in the imperative mode. This means the filling of the Spirit—whatever it is—isn't an optional part of the Christian life. Every Christian is to be filled with the Spirit all the time. If you aren't, you are out of God's will.

3. It Is in the Present Tense

This insight is particularly helpful because the Greek present tense has the idea of continual action. It's what happens when you tell your children to go out and rake the leaves before the snow comes. They go outside, rake for a few minutes, and then come back in. When you check their work, you see that most of the leaves haven't been touched. So you say, "Why didn't you rake the leaves?" "We did." "Why didn't you rake all the leaves?" "You didn't tell us to." What do you do? You tell them, "Go back, pick up the rake, and keep on raking until all the leaves are raked." That's the present tense. You keep on doing something. It's not a one-time event.

We could legitimately translate this verse this way: "Be continually filled with the Holy Spirit." That is why the filling of the Spirit is not primarily an experience. It's supposed to be the normal way of life for the Christian.

4. It Is in the Passive Voice

This is a nuance many people would miss. In Greek as in English, commands can be either active or passive. However, we're much more used to active commands: "Go to the store and pick up some milk, please." That's an active command. If I say, "Fill that hole with dirt," that's also in the active voice. But Ephesians 5:18 is in the passive voice. He doesn't say, "Fill yourself with the Spirit" but rather "Be filled with the Spirit." That's a bit hard to understand. It's like saying to someone, "Be loved." How do you "be loved"? But this is the key to everything. To "be filled" means that the filling of the Spirit is a work of God, not man.

Let me illustrate. Suppose I command you to "be loved." If there's not someone who wants to love you, you can't obey that command. Likewise, if there's not someone who wants to fill you, you can't "be filled" with the Spirit. He's not saying "fill yourself" but rather "be filled." It's exactly like the difference between saying "love yourself" and "be loved."

I draw two important implications from this truth:

1. The Holy Spirit is ready and willing to fill us at any moment.
2. The most important thing we can do is to make ourselves available to him.

That's why the New Living Translation says, "Let the Holy Spirit fill and control you." I cannot "be loved." But I can make myself available to those who want to love me. That is, I can put myself in a position of loveability. I can do those things that make me easy to love, or I can be a blockhead and make myself hard to love.

Perhaps making up a word will help us understand the concept. The word is "fillability." It's what happens when you go to a full-service gas station and say, "Fill 'er up." The person pumping the gas knows that the statement "Fill 'er up" means two things: (1) I'm empty, and (2) I want my car to be filled with gas. That's fillability. It's need plus desire. When your need to be filled with the Spirit becomes your great desire, you will be filled. Over and over again. Instantly. Every time.

Application to Life

This study of Ephesians 5:18 tells us what the filling of the Spirit is, but we still need to know how to make it a reality in our lives. There are three issues we need to think about relating to the filling of the Holy Spirit.

1. The Issue of Control

This is always the central issue of life. Who's in control of your life? Either God is in control or you are in control. But if I'm in control, then God isn't, and my life will be a mess. If God is in control, even if my circumstances seem out of control, I can still live in peaceful contentment. Either God is God or I am God. Everything else flows from that simple truth. Learn that and you've learned the central reality of life. Miss that and nothing else makes sense. Most of us need to relearn it a thousand times because it's easy to forget.

Here's a simple definition of the filling of the Spirit. *It's what happens when the Holy Spirit has the controlling interest in your life.* Go back to the contrast between wine and the Spirit. Drunken and Spirit-filled people have this in common: They are both controlled people. Their lives and their behavior are radically changed by that which fills them.

- If a person is filled with anger, than anger controls his life.
- If a person is filled with greed, then greed dominates his life.
- If a person is filled with love, then love influences all he does.

When the Holy Spirit fills you, he will have the controlling interest in your life. It is "control by consent."

At this point we need to make a critical distinction: Being filled with the Holy Spirit doesn't mean I have more of the Spirit; it means the Spirit has more of me. It doesn't happen all at once any more than you get drunk all at once. Being filled with the Spirit happens as you continually choose to live under his influence.

2. The Issue of Cooperation

While discussing this issue, a friend made an observation I had never heard before. He believes that every Christian is filled with the Spirit from the moment of the new birth. After I thought about it, it made perfect sense. Since the Holy Spirit indwells us from the moment we are saved, it follows that new believers are filled with that same Spirit, which is why new believers often have so much joy and walk so closely with the Lord. For them, it's the natural thing to do. They haven't learned to be boring and backslidden yet.

My friend then made a further very helpful comment. He said that over the years he has come to realize that for him the central issue is one of cooperation. Am I going to cooperate with the Holy Spirit and let him lead me, or I am going to keep on trying to do things my own way? So many of us struggle at precisely this point. We fight the Lord because we want to do things our way. And God says, "Okay, we can do it your way for a while, but it's not going to work." In that sense, if we won't cooperate with God, he'll cooperate with us by letting us do things in our own strength and by our own will. But then we fail and cry out to the Lord and he says, "Are you willing to cooperate with me now?"

3. The Issue of Contact

Finally, there is the issue of contact. In one of his books F. B. Meyer explained the Spirit's filling this way: Most people think of the Spirit as a substance to fill us, like gas filling up a tank. So we run out of the Spirit and God fills us again. But that's not the best image to use. In Chicago we have elevated trains that carry thousands of people to and from work each day. Those trains run on three rails—

two for the wheels and one for the electricity. The electricity is always there, but the train doesn't move unless there is contact with the third rail. Touch that rail and the train moves; pull away from the rail and it stops.

The third rail is like the Holy Spirit. His power is always available—and unlike the electric company, there's never a power shortage and never a brownout. But sometimes we live out of contact with his power. When that happens, our lives simply stop working the way God intended.

Our Greatest Need

Let me end where I began. I started by saying that the filling of the Spirit is the most important doctrine of the spiritual life. It is foundational to everything else. There is nothing we need more. Here is my final definition of the filling of the Spirit: *It is that state in which the Holy Spirit is free to do all that he came into my life to do.* The key word is *state*. The filling of the Spirit is not primarily an emotional experience and it's certainly not reserved for a few super-Christians. It's nothing more than the normal Christian life when the Holy Spirit is in control. That is why the command is in the present tense:

We are to continually be

- controlled by the Spirit,
- cooperating with the Spirit, and
- in contact with the Spirit.

This, then, is God's moment-by-moment provision for vitality, strength, courage, boldness, victory, and the abundant life. It's for you, it's a command, and it's God's plan for your life.

Emptiness and Openness

Here is some good news. God is ready, willing, and able to fill you right now. He's more willing to fill you than you are to be filled. If for some reason you aren't filled with the Holy Spirit, it's not because of God's reluctance. We do not have to beg God to do what he has already promised to do. Rather, he is begging us to make the way clear so he can do what he promised to do!

In a sense, being filled with the Spirit is an impossibility—at least as far as it depends on us. Only God's Spirit can fill us. We need two things—emptiness and openness. You can't fill a jar that's already full, and you can't fill a jar that is not open. There must be a sense of need: "Lord, I'm empty and I need to be filled by your Spirit." There must be a willingness: "Lord, I'm open to you. Let your Spirit fill me now."

The filling of the Spirit is really as simple as that. As long as we are conscious of our need and as long as we are willing to yield to the Lord, we can be filled with the Spirit all day long. This power is available to us twenty-four hours a day.

Eighty-Six Sins

Bill Bright, the founder of Campus Crusade for Christ, says that unconfessed sin grieves the Holy Spirit and that Christians can never experience the Spirit's blessing until they have dealt with sin in their lives. He suggests taking a piece of paper and writing down the sins that the Lord brings to mind, listing each one individually. Then sit in silence for a period of time, asking God to show you anything else that displeases him. Whatever the Lord shows you, write it down. It takes courage to do this, but God will always answer the sincere prayer of a penitent child of God. When you are finished, write the words of 1 John 1:7 across the sheet of paper: "The blood of Jesus, his Son, purifies us from all sin." Then take the paper and destroy it.

One Sunday morning I went to church early, determined to follow that advice. As I sat down at my desk, I pulled out a sheet of white paper and began to write down my sins, faults, shortcomings—listing every area of life that I knew to be displeasing to the Lord. I opened my heart before the Lord and wrote down everything he brought to mind. My pen flew across the paper as the Lord showed me many things in my life that displeased him. Some were sins of omission, things I should have done that I neglected to do. Others were wrong attitudes, hasty words, a tendency toward thoughtless chatter, and a streak of unkindnesses toward those I love the most.

Within thirty-six minutes, I had filled an entire page in two and a half columns. I discovered that I had written down eighty-six specific areas of my life that needed change. As I studied the list, I found that these were not eighty-six independent sins, but rather many were variations on a theme, most of them related in one way or another to the classic seven deadly sins of pride, greed, sloth, gluttony, envy, anger, and lust. It wasn't a pretty list, but I didn't feel depressed when I read it. Instead, I felt liberated and almost exhilarated, as if an enormous load had been lifted from my shoulders.

So this is the truth about Ray Pritchard! Indeed it is. And I say with the saints of all ages that in me—that is, in my flesh—dwells no good thing. Apart from the grace of God at work in my life, I am a sinner lost and undone. My heart is deceitful and wicked (Jer. 17:9). I do not know the half of my sinfulness. When the list was complete, I wrote across it in big red letters the word FORGIVEN!!! Underneath I wrote 1 John 1:7. After sharing this story with my congregation, I destroyed the list that afternoon without showing it to anyone else.

But once having done that exercise, I found it very easy to pray in faith for the filling of the Holy Spirit. I also found it easy to believe that God had answered my prayer. If you have never made such a moral inventory of your life, I encourage you to do so as soon as you finish reading this chapter.

Christ at Home in My Heart

As I think about the filling of the Spirit and the need to be open to the Lord, my mind is drawn to the familiar picture of the heart as a beautiful house with many rooms. All of us have special rooms that we reserve for entertaining our guests. Most of us also have closets, basements, and attics that we try to keep out of public view because they are messy or contain items we don't want others to see. The same is true in the spiritual realm. Many of us have welcomed Christ into a large part of our hearts. But there are areas of life where he is not welcome to enter. We have rooms in our hearts that are marked "Off Limits." It might be the kitchen or the bedroom or the recreation room that we keep locked from public view. Usually there is some hidden sin—anger or bitterness or greed or lust or theft or jealousy or promiscuous behavior—that we would be ashamed for the Lord Jesus to see. Perhaps we don't want him rearranging that part of our lives. Perhaps we like things as they are. But we will never be happy and Christ will never be fully at home until every door is opened to him.

If you want to know the power of the Spirit, the price is simple but not easy to pay. You must open those hidden doors and allow the Lord Jesus to come in and make all things new. Will it be painful? Perhaps, but the hardest part is opening the doors one by one. If you have the courage to let Christ into every part of your life, he will come in and redecorate your life into something more beautiful than you ever imagined possible.

But you'll never experience that for yourself until you start opening those doors one by one. May God help us to unlock every door and open every hidden closet until Christ is fully at home in our hearts.

If we live another day without the Holy Spirit's control in our lives, we have only ourselves to blame. God has made himself fully available to us. Have we made ourselves fully available to him?

A Truth to Remember:

If for some reason you aren't filled with the Holy Spirit, it's not because of God's reluctance.

Going Deeper

1. On a scale of 1 to 10 (lowest to highest), how would you rank your own knowledge of the Holy Spirit? On a similar scale, how would you rank your church's knowledge of the Holy Spirit?

2. Many people believe that we are living in a day when the Holy Spirit has been "rediscovered" by the church. What signs do you see that suggest this might be true? What would a "Spirit-filled church" look like?

3. Do you agree that being filled with the Spirit should be the normal experience of every Christian? If it's true, why aren't more Christians filled with the Spirit?

4. In what ways have you experienced the Holy Spirit's work in your life in the last seven days?

5. Read the list of the fruits of the Spirit in Galatians 5:22–23. Which qualities are most evident in your life? Which ones are least evident?

6. Name three ways your life would change if you were truly filled with and controlled by the Holy Spirit.

Taking Action

Set aside time to take the kind of moral and spiritual inventory mentioned in this chapter. List your sins, weaknesses, and short-comings as God brings them to mind. When you are finished, write over the list "Forgiven!" and "1 John 1:7." Then destroy or discard the list. Ask God to fill you with his Holy Spirit so that he might be in control of your life.

Chapter 5

HOW CAN I DISCOVER GOD'S WILL FOR MY LIFE?

Have you ever wished you could sit down with Jesus and talk with him about your own life? Wouldn't you like to ask him, "Lord, what do you want me to do?" All of us have moments when we want to hear God's voice or receive some definite sign regarding a relationship, a business decision, a career choice, or a major expenditure. Before we decide, we would like to know that what we are doing is what God wants us to do.

Our decisions really do matter. We make our decisions, and our decisions turn around and make us. We face so many questions:

- Should I get married? If the answer is yes, should I marry Joe or Jake or Susan or Sally?
- Should I go to college? If the answer is yes, should I go to Penn State or Georgia Tech or UCLA?
- I've been offered a new job. It's a good job. But I've got a good job. Should I take the new job? Or should I stay where I am?
- We have two children. We're thinking about having a third. Should we have another one? Or should we think about adopting?

- Is God calling me to the mission field? How can I be sure? Three mission boards are interested in me. How do I know which one to choose?

Every spring, high school seniors wrestle with the big question, "What do I do when I graduate?" And every year I write recommendations for students applying to various Christian colleges and state universities. I enjoy talking with students about their career choices and helping them take that all-important next step. Once the applications are turned in, the waiting game begins. And so does the inner turmoil. "Which colleges will accept me? Which ones will say no? What if three say yes, but my personal favorite says no? What if my favorite says yes, but I can't afford it?" What do you do then? Is there any way to be 100 percent certain about God's will when you are choosing a college?

I think it would be a lot easier if you could simply open the door one evening and be greeted by a chorus of angels chanting, "Georgia Tech! Georgia Tech! Georgia Tech!" Or if you got a special delivery letter from heaven that said, "Dear Beth, go to Wheaton. Love, God." That would make it easy. But it doesn't often happen that way. Most of the time we research, study, narrow the options, talk it over with trusted friends, pray about it, wait on the Lord, turn in our applications, and then in the end, we make our choice and hope for the best.

It's God's Responsibility, Not Ours

That raises the central issue for most people regarding God's will. We would like someone else to make the decision for us. If God would only tell us what he wanted in a given situation, we would do it. But most of the time we're left with something less than 100 percent certainty. I'm going to tell you up front that I don't believe there is any way for you to get 100 percent certainty before you sign on the dotted line. I think you can get 95 percent probability sometimes, but that's about as good as most of us will ever do in the decisions of life.

Rarely will we be absolutely certain, sometimes we will be mostly certain, and occasionally we will be downright confused as we come to the moment when we have to decide. That seems to be the case, no matter how much we have prayed and waited on the Lord. Certainty in decision making is hard to come by in a fallen world.

It helps to remember that even if we are confused, God is not. Confusion is not a sin, especially if it causes you to trust in the Lord with all your heart. Everything else in this chapter is based on the following statement: Since God wants you to know his will more than you want to know it, he takes personal responsibility to see that you discover it. *Knowing God's will is ultimately God's responsibility, not yours.* Let that last thought sink into your mind for a moment. You may never have heard it put that way before.

Let me suggest what this really means:

- He can put you exactly where he wants you to be.
- He can arrange all the details years in advance.
- He can open doors that seem shut tight.
- He can remove any obstacle that stands in your way.
- He can take your choices and fit them into his plan so that you end up in the right place at just the right time.
- He can even take your mistakes and bring good out of them.
- He can take tragedy and use it for your good and his glory.

All he needs—in fact the only thing he requires—is a willing heart. He just needs you to cooperate with him. This doesn't mean that you won't have to make decisions. But it does take the pressure off, because it means that you can trust God to take your decisions and use them to accomplish his will in your life.

Four Verses from Proverbs

While reading through the Book of Proverbs, I was repeatedly struck with the strong emphasis on the sovereignty of God over our personal decisions. Let's take a quick look at four verses that help us see how God works in, with, through, and sometimes in spite of our decisions to accomplish his will in us.

"In his heart a man plans his course, but the LORD determines his steps" (Prov. 16:9). Consider the word *determines.* This verse doesn't say that God "directs" our steps (although that is true—see Prov. 3:6 KJV), but rather that God *determines* our steps. This is a very strong word that speaks of God's control of every detail in the universe. Perhaps you've heard it said that "man proposes, but God disposes." You can make all your plans; in fact, you can have your life mapped out step by step, but in the end God determines every step you take. After we have made our plans, we don't know if they will succeed, if they should succeed, or even if we would be happier if they succeeded or failed. Our plans change because we change, our circumstances change, and the people around us change. How comforting to know that in the midst of our confusion, God determines the steps we take.

"The lot is cast into the lap, but its every decision is from the LORD" *(Prov. 16:33).* Most of us don't understand the concept of "casting lots." In the Old Testament, the Jews often used this method to determine God's will. It sometimes involved using different colored balls or rocks, mixing them together, and then seeing which one fell out of the bag first. In that sense casting lots is like rolling dice. It appears to be a random act of chance. But God is behind those colored stones. He determines which one falls out of the bag first. This means that there are no "accidents" in life, no "random" events, and there is no such thing as "luck." Even seemingly meaningless things fit into his plan. We might paraphrase the verse like this: "Life is like a roll of the dice, but God is in charge of how the numbers come up."

"Many are the plans in a man's heart, but it is the LORD'*s purpose that prevails" (Prov. 19:21).* Here's another street-level paraphrase: "You can make all the plans you like, but God gets the last word." His purpose always prevails. Some translations say that God's purpose will stand. Most of our plans don't stand. They are like the leaves that blow away in the autumn wind. But when God determines to do something, you can write it down and take it to the bank. You can make all the speeches you want and announce your long-range plans, your ten-year goals, and your personal objectives, but just remember this: When you are finished, God always gets the last word.

One of the greatest examples of this truth comes from the life of Joseph in the Old Testament. His brothers sold him to the Midianites who took him to Egypt, where through an amazing chain of events he rose to become Pharaoh's right-hand man. From that lofty position he was able to rescue his whole family during a famine in Canaan. Looking back on all that had transpired, Joseph saw the hand of God in everything that happened: "You intended to harm me, but God intended it for good to accomplish what is now being done, the saving of many lives" (Gen. 50:20). He understood that God can take the foolish choices we make and he can bring something good out of them.

"A man's steps are directed by the LORD*. How then can anyone understand his own way?" (Prov. 20:24).* There is something hidden in the Hebrew text that you wouldn't know simply from reading the English translation. The word translated "man's" in the first phrase comes from a Hebrew word that refers to a mighty warrior, a ruler, or a potentate. Solomon means to say that even the steps of a mighty man are ordained by God. The word *anyone* in the second phrase comes from the generic word for humanity. The meaning is, "If God directs the steps of the mighty, how then can an ordinary man understand his own way?"

The answer is, he can't! That's the whole point of the verse. We're like a man stumbling around in the darkness, bumping into things, tripping over ourselves, trying to find our way forward. We can't say for sure where we've come from, where we are right now, or where we're going to be tomorrow. Or we're like passengers on an overnight flight to Europe. You have to place your life in the hands of the flight crew while the plane hurtles through the night seven miles above the water. You can't be sure where you are, where you've been, or where you're going. If you look outside the plane, you can't see a thing. And since you can't do anything about it, you might as well get some sleep. Only God sees the big picture of life.

When we get up in the morning, we don't know what the day will bring. And often we don't even know what to pray for. Our uncertainty is meant to teach us daily dependence on God. He can handle the details. Our job is to trust him.

If we take these four verses together, they paint a high view of God's involvement in the details of life. His plans cannot be thwarted, but he easily frustrates the plans we make. It is right and good that we should plan for the future, but God is the one who ordains the steps we take. Our vision of the future is so limited that we can barely see the next step in front of us, and sometimes we're wrong about that. These verses remind us that we can fight against God's plan and fail, or we can cooperate with him and succeed.

Several years ago, while I was teaching through Ecclesiastes, the Lord impressed a very simple principle on my heart. It is so basic that I call it the First Rule of the Spiritual Life. Understand this rule and you will have peace in the midst of confusing circumstances. If you forget it, nothing in life will make sense to you. This is where all true understanding must begin.

The First Rule of the Spiritual Life: He's God and We're Not!

When we forget that rule, we think that we're in control of our own life and that everything depends on us. So we obsess, we hyperventilate, we try to control everything and everyone around us, we worry over all our decisions, and we spend hours fussing over the minutiae of life. What a relief to realize that God is God and you're not. Now you can rip that big "G" off your sweatshirt. You don't have to play God anymore, and you don't have to try to control everything around you. One night Corrie ten Boom was having trouble going to sleep because she was so worried about the affairs of her life. She tried praying, but it didn't help. Finally the Lord said to her, "Go to sleep, Corrie. I'm going to be up all night anyway." We ought to sleep well when we realize that God is God and he can be trusted to run the universe (including our little portion) properly.

Four Principles for Seeking God's Will

With that as background, we still need to think about the decisions of life. If God is God (and we're not!), what do we do when we are standing at the crossroads and wondering which way we should go? Here are four simple principles that can help you as you seek to do God's will.

Principle #1: Use All Your Resources to Make Wise Decisions

Sometimes people talk as if you shouldn't use your brain at all, but should wait for some mystical sign from God. The Bible does say, "Lean not on your own understanding" (Prov. 3:5), but that doesn't mean to throw your brain away. It simply means that after doing all your research on a given decision, submit it to God and ask for his help. Acts 16:6–10 offers a clear example in this regard. It tells of Paul's attempts to preach the gospel in various parts of Asia Minor (modern-day Turkey). As doors kept closing, Paul and his team ended up in Troas, near the coast of the Aegean Sea. There Paul had a vision of a man from Macedonia asking for his help. Verse 10 says that after the vision, the team discussed all the circumstances and concluded that God had called them to take the gospel to Greece. It was a combination of circumstances, plus a vision, plus a discussion of the facts that led them to a united conclusion.

This is how God usually works. We must consider open doors, closed doors, advice from others, wisdom gathered from the Scriptures, our own past experiences, plus the "still, small voice" of the Lord speaking to us. And then we must weigh everything prayerfully and carefully before deciding what we will do.

If you need to make a major decision, don't wait for the angels to knock on your door. Use your head, study the situation, gather the facts, talk to your friends, seek godly counsel, and then submit it all to the Lord.

Principle #2: Since You Can't Know the Future, You'll Rarely Have 100 Percent Certainty about Most Decisions

I've already mentioned that this may be the greatest stumbling block for some people because we would all like to be 100 percent certain before we sign on the dotted line. And some Christians believe it is wrong to be less than 100 percent certain. I can understand their thinking. After all, if you are facing a life-changing decision—a potential marriage, a cross-country move, a new career, which college to attend, whether or not to begin chemotherapy—you'd like to know in advance beyond any doubt that you are doing what God wants you to do. All too often that leaves us paralyzed by an inability to make up our minds. Some decisions are so important they can't be left to chance. As the popular saying goes, "When in doubt, don't." If you aren't sure about the new job, don't take it, don't make the move, don't say yes, don't make any decision with less than total certainty.

But is that good advice? Is it realistic? Is that the way God normally works?

- Did Noah know all about the flood? No, but he built the ark anyway.
- Did Abraham have a road map? No, but he left Ur of the Chaldees anyway.

- Did Moses know he was going to have to part the Red Sea in order to escape Egypt? No, but he led the people to the edge of the water anyway.
- Did Joshua know how the walls were going to come tumbling down? No, but he marched around Jericho anyway.
- Did Gideon fully grasp God's plan to defeat the Midianites? No, he doubted it from the beginning, but God delivered his people anyway.
- Did young David know for certain that he could defeat Goliath? No, but he picked up the five smooth stones anyway.
- Did Jehoshaphat know how God was going to defeat the Ammonites? No, but he put the singers at the front of the army and sent them out to battle anyway.

We could add dozens of other examples from the Bible. Did Esther know what would happen when she went in to see King Xerxes? Did the three Hebrew children know how they would be delivered? Was Daniel totally sure the lions would be happy to see him? Did Peter know he could walk on water? Did Paul know what would happen when he finally got to Rome?

The answer is always no. The life of faith means living with uncertainty even in the midst of doing God's will. That's the whole point of Hebrews 11. Those great men and women didn't know the future, but they trusted God anyway, sometimes in the face of great personal suffering. And because they kept on believing when circumstances turned against them, they received a great reward.

Too many people want what God has never promised—100 percent certainty before they will act. So they wait and wait and they dilly and they dally and they stop and they hesitate and they ruminate. They refuse to go forward because they are waiting for a level of confidence that almost removes the need for faith altogether. After all, if you were truly 100 percent certain, why would you need faith at all?

Principle #3: God Wants Guidable People Who Will Trust Him with the Details of Life

Guidable people look to God and not to themselves. That is, they understand that after they have done all they can, it is the Lord's purpose that prevails. Like young Samuel, they say, "Speak, for your servant is listening" (1 Sam. 3:10). Like Isaiah they cry out, "Here am I. Send me!" (Isa. 6:8)." Like the Lord Jesus they pray, "Not as I will, but as you will" (Matt. 26:39).

Let me share a secret with you. Guidable people always receive guidance from God. Always. Why? Because God always speaks loud enough for a willing ear to hear. Sometimes I talk with Christians who admit they want what they want and it doesn't matter to them what God wants. In those cases I have no advice to give. Why bother seeking God's will if what you really want is a rubber stamp on your own desires? But if you find yourself not willing to do God's will, are you willing to be made willing? That's a useful prayer if you can say it from your heart: "Lord, right now I'm not sure I want to do your will. But I am willing to be made willing. Do whatever is necessary to change my heart. Amen." God honors that kind of honesty and responds to anyone whose heart is open to him.

Are you a guidable Christian? Or do you feel like you have to be in the driver's seat of life? Are you willing to say, "Lord, let your will be done even if it means that my will is not done"?

Principle #4: When the Time Comes, Make the Best Decision You Can and Leave the Results with God

This follows from everything else I've shared in this chapter. When the time to decide comes, when you've thought about it, prayed about it, talked it over, sought godly counsel, researched your options, looked at the circumstances, searched the Scriptures, and waited on the Lord—when you've done everything you know how to do and the moment of truth comes—take a deep breath, close your eyes if you need to, and then go ahead and make the best decision you can make. I've purposely written that as a long sentence because it describes how most of our decisions are made. We wait and wait and wait and then we finally decide. And even then, we still have to trust the Lord with the results. He's God and we're not. His purposes will stand.

Make your plans. Submit them to God. Be bold when you need to be bold. Don't be afraid to decide. Leave room for God to change your plans at any time. Then trust God with the results.

I've already said that he wants you to know his will more than you want to know it. Knowing God's will is his responsibility, not yours. That means it is God's responsibility to show you his will, to guide you in the right path, to give you everything you need, and to then enable you to do his will. All you have to do is trust him with the details of your life.

A friend shared this thought with me: "God has enough trouble getting us to do his will, without making it hard to find." I believe that's true. If you are willing to be guided by God, you will discover that he will lead you step by step by step. In the end you will be what he wants you to be, you will go where he wants you to go, and you will do what he wants you to do. This is God's promise to guidable Christians who are willing to do his will.

The Twenty-One-Day Challenge

Recently my wife and I had lunch with some friends who were visiting from a distant city. As we began our meal, the thought passed through my mind that the husband looked more relaxed than I had seen him in a long time. I soon discovered the reason for his calm demeanor. He told me about a simple prayer he had been praying at the beginning of each new day. He heard a noted Christian leader suggest using this prayer for twenty-one days. My friend said that he had tried it and that the prayer had made a profound difference in his life. At that point his wife chimed in to say that she had noticed a drastic difference in him as well. Before he started praying the prayer, he often came home tense over things that had happened to him during the day. But now he comes home relaxed and in a good mood.

As I listened, I wondered to myself what kind of magic prayer could make that kind of difference. My friend said that for him the key is to pray the prayer the moment he wakes up—even before he gets out of bed. He even said that he had awakened that morning at 4:30 A.M., so he prayed the prayer and then went back to sleep.

The prayer itself is the essence of simplicity. It goes like this: *"Heavenly Father, you are in charge of everything that will happen to me today—whether it be good or bad, positive or negative. Please make me thankful for everything that happens to me today. Amen."*

This prayer is powerful because it doesn't change anything outside of me, but it does change everything inside of me. My circumstances don't change, but my attitude does. And that's why my friend looked so relaxed when we ate lunch.

Perhaps you need to take the twenty-one-day challenge. Pray that simple prayer first thing in the morning for the next twenty-one days and see what happens in your heart.

Life is a mysterious journey, full of unexpected twists and turns. The path ahead is a mystery to us all. No one can say for sure what is around the next bend. It may be a smooth road through a lovely valley, or we may discover that the bridge is washed out and we have to find a way to cross a deep river. Often the road will seem to disappear, or it may suddenly seem to go in three different directions and we won't know which way to go. But there is One who knows the way because the past, present, and future are all the same to him and the darkness is as the light of day. He knows the way we should go. He promised to direct your path, and he will do it. You can count on it.

A Truth to Remember:
**If you are truly willing to do God's will,
you will do it.**

Going Deeper

1. Sometimes tiny decisions turn out to have huge consequences. Can you think of a time when a spur-of-the-moment decision ended up changing your life?

2. "Knowing God's will for your life is God's responsibility, not yours." What does that statement mean? Do you agree or disagree?

3. "It is rarely God's will to give you 100 percent certainty before you make an important decision." Have you ever come to a major decision and taken a step of faith in spite of your personal doubts? What happened?

4. Read the four verses from Proverbs mentioned in this chapter. Which one seems to apply most directly to your life right now?

5. Name a time in your life when God took a mistake you made and brought something good out of it. What did you learn about God and about yourself from that experience?

6. Why is it important that we pray "Lord, let your will be done even if it means that my will is not done"? What happens inside us when we refuse to pray that prayer? In what area of your life do you need to pray that prayer right now?

Taking Action

This chapter mentions a prayer that someone prayed as part of a twenty-one-day challenge: *"Heavenly Father, you are in charge of everything that will happen to me today—whether it be good or bad, positive or negative. Please make me thankful for everything that happens to me today. Amen."* Try praying this prayer first thing in the morning for the next three weeks and see what difference it makes in your life.

Chapter 6

HOW CAN I LEARN TO PRAY?

This chapter is for anyone who would like to know how to pray more effectively. I suppose on one level that includes everyone, because if you pray at all, you probably wish you knew more about it. The paradox of prayer is that it is a joyful burden for most of us. Like the disciples, we want to say, "Lord, teach us to pray." Those are words we would say even if we have been praying for many years.

Many Christians feel guilty because we know deep inside that we do almost every part of the Christian life better than we pray. We give our money and our time, we go to church, we support missionaries, we witness for Christ, we read good books, and we try to be obedient to the Lord. And still prayer is difficult even after years of practice and dozens of sermons telling us how to pray. I have no desire to add to your guilt. It won't help you for me to add to your burden. My goal is to increase your joy by showing you the boundless possibilities of prayer.

Not long ago my wife and I ate supper with another couple at a steak house in New Port Richey, Florida. The husband directs a Bible conference center where I was speaking that week. During our conversation he mentioned that prayer was the one area of the spiritual life where he struggles the most. Even though he gets up at 5:30 A.M. every day to pray and read his Bible, he still feels this is an area where he needs more growth. As I reflected on his words, it occurred to me that my friend is one of the most godly men I know. He has a walk with God that is obvious to all who know him, and his integrity is beyond reproach. Yet he said what I would say and what most Christian leaders would say. We all wish we were stronger in the area of prayer.

There are at least three things that hinder us from going deeper in prayer. The first is the sneaking suspicion that prayer doesn't matter. It's easy to fall into a kind of fatalism that says, "God's gonna do what God's gonna do." So we stop praying because we think nothing will change. Then there is the fear that we won't pray in the "right" way, that we won't use the correct words or we won't use the right formula and that God therefore won't even bother to hear what we say. And most of us struggle with the little voice inside that tells us we've got more important things to do. Prayer is good, but we need to get on with the "real business" of the day. (And it doesn't necessarily help when we hear that story about Martin Luther saying he had to get up at 4:00 A.M so he could pray two extra hours because he was facing an extra-busy day. That's just one more way we're not like Luther.) So we don't pray as we ought or as we would like.

Keep On Asking!

Rather than deal with those hindrances, let me simply share some very good news: *God welcomes prayer*. He wants us to pray, he begs us to pray, he exhorts us to pray, and he pleads with us to pray. Prayer is God's appointed means for us to receive what we need from him.

As Jesus was coming to the end of the Sermon on the Mount, he laid out the most basic teaching on prayer in the New Testament. In the familiar words of Matthew 7:7, Jesus tells us to ask, seek, and knock. "Ask and it will be given to you; seek and you will find; knock and the door will be opened to you." Those three verbs are in the present tense in the Greek language. You could legitimately translate them this way: Keep on asking, keep on seeking, and keep on knocking at the door. This means that prayer requires persistence. Few prayers are answered the first time we pray them. But God's delays do not mean he doesn't care. We are to ask, ask, and keep on asking. We are to seek, seek, and keep on seeking. We are to knock, knock, and keep on knocking. If we do, we will receive, find, and the door will be opened to us.

What Jesus is teaching us about prayer can be summarized in three statements:

1. God wants to answer our prayers.
2. Our prayers will be answered but not immediately.
3. We should lay aside our doubts and continue to pray because of who God is.

The words of Walt Gerber are a great encouragement at this point: "Remember, when praying for others, we are not overcoming God's reluctance, but laying hold of his highest willingness."[7]

Three Levels of Prayer

These famous words of Jesus describe three levels of prayer. Not all prayer is alike in its basic nature. Sometimes we are asking, sometimes we are seeking, and sometimes our prayers are like knocking at the door of heaven.[8]

Level 1: Asking

"Ask and it will be given to you. . . . For everyone who asks receives" (Matt. 7:7–8). Go to Africa or India and you will understand what this means. Asking is what beggars do. In poor countries, beggars unashamedly stand by the road with their hands held out, asking

alms for the poor. Sometimes they can be quite bold about it and even irritating to passersby. In those moments it helps to remember that you would be bold too if you were in their position. Jesus tells us that prayer begins with the posture of a beggar coming before a benevolent heavenly Father. We are to ask God for what we need, knowing that he is able to help us. The promise is very simple: Ask and you shall receive.

Level-one praying involves the basic needs of life. If you need food, ask God for it. If you need money to pay the bills, ask God for it. If you need wisdom, if you need guidance, if you are confused, if you are in need of physical healing, do not be ashamed or embarrassed to bring your needs to the Lord in your prayers. This is what it means to ask God for "daily bread." Asking involves laying all of life before the Lord in order that you might receive from him whatever you need.

Notice how broad the promise is. It extends to "everyone who asks." And see how definite the promise is. Everyone who asks "receives." Not "shall receive" or "might receive" or "may receive" but simply "receives."

Prayer begins with asking God for what we need, knowing that when we ask, we will receive an answer from heaven.

Level 2: Seeking

"Seek and you will find. . . . He who seeks finds" (Matt. 7:7–8). Seeking implies a desire for something of great value. It reminds us of Jesus' story of the woman searching for a lost coin or the shepherd with one hundred sheep who, having lost one, left the ninety-nine and went searching for the one sheep that had gone astray. It is like a man seeking a pearl of great price who, having found it, gives all that he has in order to purchase it.

When you seek something, you rearrange your priorities so that you can search for what you desire until you find it. This kind of prayer is usually tied up with the search for deeper understanding, particularly as it applies to the trials of life. In 2 Corinthians 12 we learn about Paul's "thorn in the flesh." We don't know what it was because Paul doesn't tell us. It might have been a physical ailment or it could have been fierce opposition from his Jewish critics. Three times he asked the Lord to remove it, and three times the Lord said no. That's the first level of prayer—asking. But he kept on praying for insight, and God eventually said, "My grace is sufficient for you, for my power is made perfect in weakness" (2 Cor. 12:9).

This is level-two praying—seeking wisdom from the Lord. While the thorn was not removed (and evidently was never removed), Paul gained important spiritual insight that helps us see why his first prayers were not answered. This kind of answer comes only as we repeatedly seek the Lord.

Level 3: Knocking

"Knock and the door will be opened to you. . . . And to him who knocks, the door will be opened" (Matt. 7:7–8). The word knock means to stand at a door and repeatedly rap it with your knuckles. You knock and wait, then you knock again, then you say, "I know you're in there," then you knock again and say, "I can hear your voice. Come on, open the door." Then you knock again. If you're on the other side, you know how annoying it can be to listen as someone knocks and knocks and keeps on knocking. But that's precisely the picture behind these words. They imply praying in the face of difficulty and even resistance. If you knock like this, your desire for entrance must be very great indeed. In the New Testament, the picture of "open doors" often deals with seeking God's will and praying for new opportunities to spread the gospel. It also applies to praying when the object desired involves changing the heart of another person.

Not long ago a young couple came to see me with the good news that they plan to be missionaries. They are eminently qualified and will do a wonderful job. There is only one small problem. After months of prayer, they have no idea where they would like to go. And they can't start raising support until they at least know what country they are going to. As we talked, I said something like this: "The reason you don't know now is because you don't need to know now. If you needed to know now, God would have shown you. Since you don't know now, it must be true that you don't need to know because when you do need to know, you'll know, and not one minute sooner. If God is God, that must be true." I more or less said that off the top of my head, but looking back I decided that it was good advice because it is based on the truth that God gives us guidance when we need it, and generally that guidance comes just in the nick of time.

A few days later I happened to talk with someone whose job is ending soon. This person had been praying for guidance, but no direction was coming from heaven. So I shared what I had said to the young couple. The next week I got an E-mail message telling me that she had chatted with another friend who asked, "Have you ever thought about serving overseas?" No, but she was open to the idea. Then came a "chance" meeting with a missionary representative who spoke about all the open doors in other countries. A few days later she found what seemed to be a perfect opportunity in Africa. That led to an E-mail application, references by E-mail, and a phone interview. I eventually received a message telling me that she is moving to Kenya to start a new job at a school for the children of missionaries. It's a perfect fit, and all the pieces came together at just the right time. That's how God works. We do the knocking, and in due season the door opens up for us.

Sometimes the answer is years in coming. One Sunday I was greeting people between services when a couple came up to me with their arms around each other and tears in their eyes. They asked me to pray for them because God had worked a miracle in their relationship and right now they were going through a fiery trial. I didn't know the details, but I put my arms around them and committed their marriage to God. The next Sunday the wife came up with wonderful news about how God had answered that prayer in a most remarkable way. Later I reflected on the fact that nearly eight years ago the wife had come to see me several times, asking prayer for a marriage that seemed hopeless. And now the answer had finally come from heaven.

Why do some prayers take years to be answered and others are answered immediately? I do not know the answer and find it useless to speculate. But this much is clear: if we keep on knocking at heaven's door, sooner or later the door will be opened to us.

As I look at these three levels of prayer, it strikes me that there are no limits. Anyone may pray to God about anything. And the emphasis falls not on our prayers but on the certainty of answers from God. Three times Jesus mentions our part. We are to ask, seek, and knock. But six times he tells us that we will receive, we will find, and the door will be opened to us. It is as if God is pleading and begging with us to dare to come to him in prayer. This brings to mind Billy Graham's remark that there are rooms in heaven filled with answers to prayer for which no one has thought to ask.

God's Character and Our Prayers

How can we be so sure that when we ask, seek, and knock that we will receive, find, and the door will be opened to us? Jesus says that our hope in prayer rests not with ourselves or in the power of positive thinking, but in the very character of God who is our great Father in heaven.

"Which of you, if his son asks for bread, will give him a stone? Or if he asks for a fish, will give him a snake?" (Matt. 7:9–10). Good fathers are eager to help their children. This is what fathers do. They give "good" gifts to their children. If your child asks for a stone or a snake, will you give it to him? No. What if he begs? No. What if he pleads?

No. If he says, "I can't live without that snake," you still say no. Children often ask for foolish things, which are withheld. The same is true with God. Often we plead for things that to us seem like bread but to God are like a poisonous snake. Our heavenly Father says no, not because he hates us but because he loves us. Sometimes God's no is the surest sign of his love for us. Suppose your five-year-old asks to play with a sharp knife. What will you do? You say no and let him cry and even pout. His tears show his immaturity. If you give him the knife when you know it could hurt him, you don't really love him at all.

We often ask for things that would harm us. It might be a new job or a bigger salary or a new husband or a new wife. But God sees through to the end and knows that what we have asked for would harm us more than help us. So in love he says no.

"If you, then, though you are evil, know how to give good gifts to your children, how much more will your Father in heaven give good gifts to those who ask him!" (Matt. 7:11). The argument is from the lesser to the greater, from the human to the divine. My father was not a perfect man, but I never doubted his love for me. I am not a perfect father, but I hope my boys never doubt my love for them. There is One who is much greater than I am, whose heart is pure and good, and whose love knows no limits. He is my heavenly Father, and he bids me come to him in prayer. That is the real meaning of the phrase "how much more."

- God knows much more than we do.
- God cares much more than we do.

He is richer than we are and he is far more willing to answer our prayers than we are to have them answered. But how can we be sure that God cares for us so deeply? Go with me to a hill outside Jerusalem, not far from the Damascus Gate. Look closely at the three men who are dying on bloody Roman crosses. Study that awful scene closely. Listen to the jeering crowd. Ponder the meaning of the words spoken by the man hanging on the middle cross. There you will have your answer.

We know that God loves us because he gave his own Son to die for us. And he did it unasked. He sent his Son to the earth while we were in rebellion against him, knowing that we would put him to death. Will he now refuse us any good thing we ask of him? The cross proves that the heart of God is good. And we come to that same good heart every time we pray.

The final phrase of verse 11 tells us that all the blessings of heaven are promised "to those who ask him." We should expect God to answer our prayers, and we can expect nothing without prayer. In the deepest, most profound sense God's blessings are "limited" to those who ask for them. He will not give if we do not ask. The gates of heaven open to those who pray. Those same gates are closed to everyone else.

Steve Meyer's Testimony

Let's wrap up this chapter with three simple statements:

1. The invitation to pray comes from God's heart.
2. Our doubts come from our hearts.
3. Will we believe God or ourselves?

We doubt God's goodness so we don't pray. When hard times come, we give in to worry and despair because we have forgotten how good God has been to us. A good memory of God's blessings will fortify us in the time of trouble and give us the courage to pray with thanksgiving.

At the age of forty-four, Steve Meyer was diagnosed with stage 4 mantle cell lymphoma. That's a form of cancer that eventually takes the life of almost everyone who has it. Not many people live more than five or six years after their diagnosis. For many months Steve was given heavy-duty chemotherapy in a desperate attempt to beat back the cancer and save his life. Even though his hair fell out, week after week he faithfully came to church, sometimes battling great pain. The initial results from the chemotherapy were encouraging. Many of the tumors disappeared, and others shrank dramatically.

The next step in the treatment cycle called for Steve to undergo a very difficult bone marrow transplant in which the doctors harvested his stem cells, radiated his whole body to destroy all his bone marrow, then reinserted the stem cells, all the while hoping his body could fight off infection while his immune system was temporarily disabled. Steve knew the risks and knew that he could undergo this kind of treatment only once because his body could not endure it twice. The doctors made no guarantees. The cancer could come back even after the bone marrow transplant, but that was still the best chance for a cure.

A few days before he went into the hospital, I spoke with Steve on the phone and found him to be incredibly cheerful and filled with optimism about the future. He had committed his life into God's hands and was content to leave everything with the Lord. He had also joined an E-mail list of six hundred patients around the world who have his kind of cancer. Someone wrote Steve saying they had just been diagnosed with mantle cell lymphoma and they wondered what to expect. Steve wrote back an answer that is an eloquent statement of faith. With his permission I am reproducing it here:

> I am not happy to have this disease, nor is any-
> one who has it. Chemotherapy is not a refreshment,
> bone marrow transplants are less fun than going to
> the lake in the summer. And having one's life ripped
> apart by a disease that has historically killed all its
> victims is not my first choice.
>
> On the other hand, when you are surrounded by
> people who love you, people who pray for you,
> people who bring you meals, send you cards, rake

your leaves, cry with you, laugh with you, do your chores for you, shovel your snow all winter, cut your grass all summer, come over on Sunday to watch football with you, call you on the phone, pick up your medicine for you, drive you places when you can't, offer you their homes, offer support to your husband or wife, offer support to your kids, offer support to your healthy parents, offer support to your brothers and sisters, come over to keep you company, take you out to dinner, bring you books, CDs, tapes, loan you their laptop computer, offer their friendship and love . . .

When your kids tell you they love you again and again and again and cry at the thought of losing you, when your wife or husband tells you they love you even when you act like an idiot and they cry themselves to sleep at the thought of losing you, when you see tears in your parents' eyes at the thought of losing a child to this disease and they say "I wish it were me" and they mean it . . .

When people you've never met pray for you, send you mail, encourage you, meet you for dinner, when the doctor weeps for you because he wishes he could do more, when the pain gets so bad it takes away your breath, or you get so sick you think you're gonna die . . .

I'll tell you what I do. I thank God for my life just the way it is! I have had a good life, and I intend to live for many years to come. I plan on seeing my Becky grow up. Today she was the happiest little girl in the third grade, and so proud to read her grades one by one to her dad, who she has no doubt loves her with all of his heart. I plan to see my twelve-year-old son's penmanship improve even if it takes forever, and someday he will beat me in chess. I plan to see my sophomore-in-college daughter someday grow up the rest of the way and get married and give me grandkids. I plan to see my parents finish their lives with their son alive, and I'll bury them when they die. I plan to see my beautiful wife grow old, get gray hair, and sag, so I can love her more then than I do now, and we can retire to Florida.

Did we all get a bad break? Yes.

Do we have a right to complain? A little.

Would I change my life if I could? Never.

I'm glad you asked the question, and I pray that you and everyone else with this disease gets cured, and those who have died from this disease I plan to see them again. The quality of my life has never been better!!!

May God bless all those with mantle cell lymphoma and the loving caregivers and families.

Steve Meyer
Oak Park, Illinois

"If You Know the Lord"

Over the phone Steve told me the secret of his strong faith. It consists of a simple statement that goes right to the heart of the Christian faith: "If you know the Lord, you don't need to fear dying, because if you know the Lord, you're never really dead." What an amazing statement that is. It's exactly what Jesus meant when he said, "Whoever lives and believes in me will never die" (John 11:26).

What can you do with a man like that? You can't stop him. His faith is indestructible. The devil can't touch a man like that because the devil's ultimate weapon is the fear of death. If you aren't afraid to die, then the devil has no power over you.

Herein lies a powerful secret for a dynamic prayer life. Count your blessings instead of your problems. Focus on what God has done for you instead of on how you wished things had turned out. Think of all the good things that have come into your life in the midst of your difficulties. When you remember the goodness of God, you will have no trouble asking, seeking, and knocking.

The application is simple. Keep on praying. Do not be dismayed by delay or defeated by your circumstances. Let the words of Jesus fill your heart. Ask, ask, and keep on asking and you will receive. Seek, seek, and keep on seeking, and you will find. Knock, knock, and keep on knocking, and by God's grace the door will be opened to you. This is the promise of the Lord Jesus Christ.

A Truth to Remember:
Prayer is God's appointed means for us to receive what we need from him.

Going Deeper

1. "Many Christians feel guilty because we know deep inside that we do almost every part of the Christian life better than we pray." Do you agree or disagree? How would you evaluate the level of your own prayer life?
2. What difference has prayer made in your life? Can you name a time when prayer changed your life?
3. What things fall into the "asking" category for you? What are you "seeking" from the Lord? And what doors are you praying will be opened for you?

4. The Scriptures speak often of waiting on the Lord. What spiritual benefits do we gain as we wait on the Lord for the answer to our prayers? .
5. What do we gain from praying with others?
6. Why is it important to count our blessings instead of our problems when we pray? Stop right now and name five blessings you have received from the Lord in the last seven days.

Taking Action

We all need practical ideas to help us pray more effectively. Here's a simple one. Try "Alphabet Praying" for a week. You start by praying for something or someone with the letter A, the letter B, then the letter C, and so on through the alphabet. Don't do it from a written list. Ask the Lord to bring to your mind who or what you should pray for as you come to each letter. Do this for a week and you may be surprised at the freshness that comes to your prayer life.

Chapter 7

HOW CAN I OVERCOME TEMPTATION?

Playwright Oscar Wilde once remarked jokingly, "I can resist everything except temptation." We smile when we read those words because they speak an important truth about the human condition. Temptation pays a visit to each of us every day, and most of us struggle to say no.

"What do I do when those thoughts come to me?" the young man asked. He is in his late thirties, a rising young executive, by all outward appearances the very image of success. Almost ten years ago he took his M.B.A. degree and parlayed it into a profitable career as a stockbroker. He has a good job, is well-respected by his peers, and seems to have no trouble mixing his faith and his work. What could be wrong? As a single man in a high-powered business environment, he faces numerous temptations, many coming from the sexual arena. "I've asked God to give me a Christian wife, but he hasn't answered that prayer yet. Sometimes my mind is filled with thoughts that embarrass me. And sometimes I give in to the temptation I feel."

I was not surprised. If you change the name or a few details, it was a story I had heard many times before. In fact, it is a story that is as old as the Bible itself. Temptation is not new in any sense. Temptation is the same for us as it was for Adam and Eve in the Garden of Eden. Satan tempts us today in the same way he tempted Jesus in the wilderness. From the very beginning a battle has raged for the souls of men and women, a battle that touches all of us sooner or later.[9]

It's Not a Sin to Be Tempted

Perhaps the place to begin is with the important truth that it is not a sin to be tempted. Many Christians feel needless guilt because they have equated temptation with sin. Yet we know that our Lord was tempted and was without sin (Heb. 4:15). Was the temptation real? The answer must be yes. But if the sinless Son of God could be tempted, then temptation itself cannot be sinful.

Let's suppose a young man and woman start dating. After a few weeks he confesses to his pastor that he is experiencing sexual temptation. "Why are you surprised?" the pastor replies. "It would be more surprising if you weren't being tempted." Temptation is a sign that we still live in a fallen world. It's not the temptation that matters; it's how you respond to it.

Think how many temptations you and I face in an ordinary day. Staying in bed late—the temptation to laziness. Dressing carelessly—the temptation to sloppiness. Growling at the breakfast table—the temptation to unkindness. Arguing over who should change the baby this time—the temptation to selfishness. Starting work ten minutes late—the temptation to slothfulness. Losing your temper when a coworker crashes your computer—the temptation to impatience. Flirting with that good-looking woman, taking a second look at that good-looking man—the temptation to lust. Refusing to speak to a person who has hurt you—the temptation to malice. Repeating a juicy story of your neighbor's misfortune—the temptation to gossip. Taking a secret drink at a party—the temptation to drunkenness.

Lying awake at night thinking sensual thoughts—the temptation to impurity. Taking your anger out on the children after a hard day—the temptation to cruelty. Going out to eat when you can't afford it—the temptation to self-indulgence. Having a second helping and then a third—the temptation to gluttony. Firing off a hasty letter to a friend who hurt you—the temptation to revenge.

Unseen Battles

Most of the battles we face will not be enormous, life-changing decisions, or at least they won't seem that way at the time. Either we get angry or we don't. You stay up late to finish your homework or you make up a creative excuse. When you visit the department store you pay cash or you break your promise not to use your credit card. You repeat the unkind story you heard or you decide to keep it to yourself. You pass by the magazine rack in the airport terminal or you stop and begin to browse. You get up early to exercise or you roll over for another thirty minutes of sleep.

Either way no one else will know whether you exercised or not. And no one will know (at least not until the end of the month) if you used your credit card or not. And no one will know (unless you are audited) whether or not you lied on your tax return. God has ordained that our spiritual progress should be measured not by huge battles won or lost but by a thousand daily skirmishes no one else knows about.

It is precisely at this point that 1 Corinthians 10:13 becomes so important. It's a verse every Christian should know by heart because it reveals important spiritual truth about temptation. "No temptation has seized you except what is common to man. And God is faithful; he will not let you be tempted beyond what you can bear. But when you are tempted, he will also provide a way out so that you can stand up under it." Note three truths from this verse. First, *temptation is the common experience of all Christians*. If you say, "I'll be glad when I'm not tempted," you're really saying, "I'll be glad when I'm dead" because you will be tempted as long as you are alive. Temptation changes shape across the years, but it never goes away completely. Second, *God will not allow you to be put in a situation where you have to give in to sin.* The pressure may be enormous, but he always provides a "way out" sooner or later. Third, *God's "way out" does not necessarily remove you from temptation, but it puts you in a position to endure it with grace.* Sometimes we will be tempted over and over and over again. Each time God promises to give us what we need to resist successfully.

Not long ago a friend commented that during a tense exchange with her teenage daughter, she "bit her tongue" instead of blowing her top. Every temptation—whether large or small—requires a moment-by-moment decision. When your boss asks you to fudge the figures on the monthly financial report, you have only a few seconds to decide how to respond. When you are surfing the Internet and happen to run across a site filled with pornography, you must choose immediately whether or not you'll click the mouse button. Sometimes you truly will have to bite your tongue and then bite it again to keep from sinning.

Five Principles to Help Us Resist Temptation

As we lean on the Lord, we discover that even when we are sorely pressed by the devil, God is faithful. There is always a "way out" for those who will take it. In all the Bible, there is no better example of this truth than the case of Joseph in Genesis 39. From this familiar story I find five principles that will help us in our personal struggle with the temptations of life.

Principle #1: Temptation Often Comes When We Least Expect It

The scene is the royal court of Egypt. A man by the name of Potiphar enters the room. He is the captain of Pharaoh's bodyguard, a position of great honor because he was personally responsible for the Pharaoh's safety. At his side is a young man, not an Egyptian, a fact made clear by his appearance. If you were an onlooker, you would notice the young man immediately and say, "I wonder where he came from."

He is tall, about 6'1" or perhaps an inch or two taller, ruddy, well-built, with medium-brown hair, piercing blue eyes, and that casual walk we tend to associate in young men with a high degree of self-confidence. As he follows Potiphar, all eyes follow him. He has it all—good looks, self-confidence, poise, and a playful sense of humor. His name is Joseph.

Wherever Potiphar goes, Joseph follows. They look good together, these two. Not father and son exactly. As a matter of fact, Potiphar had purchased Joseph as a slave from the Ishmaelites. So they couldn't be father and son, but they didn't seem like master and slave either. There is something else at work—a kind of friendship that stretches across the years and the culture that separates them. Potiphar, captain of Pharaoh's bodyguard, likes this young man from Israel. For his part, Joseph admires his master.

This is how Moses puts the matter: "The LORD was with Joseph and he prospered, and he lived in the house of his Egyptian master. When his master saw that the LORD was with him and that the LORD gave him success in everything he did . . ." (Gen. 39:2–3).

Potiphar was no dummy. He knew that the Lord's hand was upon this young man he had purchased as a slave. So he put Joseph in charge of his house. Verses 4–5 clearly imply that he was a wealthy man with a large estate. Notice what happens when Joseph takes over: "From the time he put him in charge of his household and of all that he owned, the LORD blessed the household of the Egyptian because of Joseph. The blessing of the LORD was on everything Potiphar had, both in the house and in the field" (Gen. 39:5).

I pause to make one simple comment: It appears as if Joseph has got it made. Sure, he was sold into slavery by his brothers, but things have really turned around. He's only eighteen or nineteen years old and now he's managing the affairs of one of the most powerful men in Egypt. Joseph is exactly where God wants him to be. Verses 2–6 emphasize over and over again that God's blessing is on his life.

How, then, does he get into such trouble? The answer is crucial. There is no contradiction between God's blessing and your temptations. We often think there is. We honestly believe that if we do what is right, we will never be tempted. But the opposite is true. We are much more likely to be tempted when things are going well for us.

Why? First, because if we are never tested when things are going well, we tend to get arrogant and big-headed. Second, Satan tempts us during our good times in order to destroy our testimony. Third, temptation often blindsides us in the moment of our greatest success because that is when we least expect it. Fourth, temptation successfully resisted prepares us to do greater things for God.

The lesson is clear. When everything is going your way . . . when you've got the world by the tail on a downhill slide . . . when you just got a promotion . . . when your popularity has never been higher . . . when your dreams start to come true . . . watch out! Be careful! Take nothing for granted! Keep your eyes open! Just because things are going well doesn't mean you're home free. Today's victories often lead to tomorrow's trials.

Principle #2: Repeated Temptation May Be Resisted, but Only by Those Who Know Who They Are

It is exactly at this point—when Joseph seems to be sitting on top of the world—that a new character enters the story. We do not know her name, only that she is the wife of Potiphar, and connected to him in name only. To use a modern phrase, she is a "single married woman."

Verse 7 lays out the situation for us with unabashed directness: "After a while his master's wife took notice of Joseph and said, 'Come to bed with me!'" The Hebrew has a wonderful way of putting it. It literally says that she "lifted up her eyes" at Joseph. The Living Bible says she began "making eyes" at him. As he crossed the room she followed him with her eyes, a smile of satisfaction crossing her face. He was a fine-looking man, young and strong the way Potiphar had been when they first met, before too many court dinners had spoiled his waistline and before too many late night meetings with Pharaoh had placed permanent bags under his eyes. Yes, this Joseph looked like an excellent companion for a casual affair, a brief meeting between a younger man and an older woman.

She must have been persistent because when Joseph turned her down (verses 8–9), she came back again and again. Perhaps she thought he didn't mean it when he said no. Perhaps she thought she could wear down his resistance. Perhaps she thought he wanted to but was afraid to say yes. Back she came, slinking into his life, offering him forbidden fruit, ripe and juicy, his for the taking. Still he said no.

At this point it's worth pausing to ask why a red-blooded young man would say no to an available woman. Verses 8 and 9 suggest two answers:

1. *He was loyal to his boss.* "'With me in charge,' he told her, 'my master does not concern himself with anything in the house; everything he owns he has entrusted to my care. No one is greater in this house than I am. My master has withheld nothing from me except you, because you are his wife'" (vv. 8–9a).

2. *He was loyal to God.* "How then could I do such a wicked thing and sin against God?" (v. 9b).

Joseph did the right thing because he knew that adultery was wrong. He called it "a wicked thing" and a "sin against God." These days we like to rename sin to make it sound less sinful. Instead of a hard word like "adultery," we use words like "affair," "tryst," "fling," "one-night stand," and we even call it "making love." Call it what you like. Adultery is still sin because God says so. Renaming sin doesn't change its character any more than calling rat poison "food" turns it into bread.[10]

Joseph knew he belonged to God. When a person knows that he belongs to God, it makes the decisions of life easier. If you belong to God, you can't sleep with your boss's wife. It's just that simple. It doesn't matter that she's lonely or attractive or available or anything else. You just can't do it. Period. End of story. No discussion needed.

- He didn't mess around.
- He didn't flirt with trouble.
- He didn't say, "How far can I go?"
- He just said no!

One final point: Joseph didn't apologize for saying no and he didn't worry about hurting her feelings.

Principle #3: God's Way of Escape Is Rarely Easy and Must Be Quickly Taken

As I pondered the matter, I made a list of excuses Joseph might have given for sleeping with Potiphar's wife:

- We're all alone (true).
- She made me do it (also true).
- No one else will know (probably true).
- She's in a bad marriage (very possible).
- I'm single and I have needs too (definitely true).
- I deserve this (not true).
- Everyone fools around (not true, but it sounds good).
- God will understand (definitely not true, but a popular excuse).

In his commentary on this text, James Montgomery Boice notes how hard Joseph tried to avoid a confrontation. First, he reasoned with Potiphar's wife, then he avoided her as much as possible, but in the end she forced the issue. It was all or nothing. Either he slept with her or he faced losing his job. The King James Version uses a quaint expression to describe how Joseph responded to the final seduction: "He left his garment in her hand, and fled, and got him out" (v. 12). Why does it say, "He got him out"? Because no one else could get him out so he got himself out of trouble.[11]

When she grabbed his coat, he made up his mind in an instant. He started running and never looked back. She's holding his coat and he's making like the Road Runner going the other way. When she said, "Why don't you stay for a while?" he said, "I'd love to, but I've got to run." And that's exactly what he did. Out the door, across the lawn, over the hedge, dodging camels as he went. He left her holding his coat while he ran the other way.

After I preached on this text, a friend came to me and said, "Pastor Ray, you need to emphasize one point even more. Tell the people they need to make up their minds in advance. If they wait until they are tempted, it will be too late." How true. What will you do when you are tempted to do that which you know is wrong? Don't wait until Potiphar's wife is playing kissy-face with you. It's too late then. Make up your mind now, before it happens, so that when it happens, you'll know exactly what to do.

- There is a time to talk and a time to stop talking.
- There is a time to stay and a time to go.
- There is a time to walk and a time to run away.

When temptation comes, you've got to move fast. God isn't obligated to give you a second chance to get out clean. He promised to make a "way out," but he isn't obligated to give you three choices in case you don't like the first two.

Principle #4: Those Who Resist Temptation Are Rarely Rewarded by the World

As you can imagine, Potiphar's wife wasn't too happy about all this. Hell hath no fury like a woman scorned. While Joseph is running half-dressed across the countryside, she's left with nothing but a handful of dirty laundry. This is not a good thing. Two things happen in short order:

1. *She makes a false accusation* (vv. 13–18). In essence, she accuses Joseph of attempted rape. When she calls him "a Hebrew" (v. 17), there is even a touch of racism in her words. Her words sound plausible because she's got Joseph's coat in her hand.

2. *Joseph is unjustly imprisoned* (vv. 19–20). The Bible says that when Potiphar heard this story, his anger burned. So he had Joseph thrown into jail with the common criminals. How could such a thing happen? It happened because the world cannot understand a believer with conviction. That's why Joseph was locked up. He knew who he was, and he acted on his convictions. His reward was a quick trip to jail.

The good news is, you can stand up to temptation. The bad news is, you may end up losing your popularity in the process. After all, the world crucified Jesus. Why should you and I expect to get off any easier?

Principle #5: God Honors Those Who Dare to Say No

Before we leave this story, we need to see how it ends. It's not the way we might have expected. "The LORD was with him; he showed him kindness and granted him favor in the eyes of the prison warden. So the warden put Joseph in charge of all those held in the prison, and he was made responsible for all that was done there. The warden paid no attention to anything under Joseph's care, because the LORD was with Joseph and gave him success in whatever he did" (Gen. 39:21–23).

Now Joseph is chained in a filthy pit (see Ps. 105:18). Because of his faithfulness to God, he lost his job, his freedom, and his reputation. He appears to be a ruined man.

This story proves that God honors those who dare to say no. It may not appear that way at first. Things may not work out exactly like we think they will. But when we have the courage to say no to temptation, God takes care of the details. In the end, we will never be disappointed. Remember, it's always better to do right the first time. There are some things worse than going to jail for doing right. One of them is living in the prison of a guilty conscience. It is better to do right and sleep well than to toss and turn because you couldn't say no.

There is a neat symmetry to this story of Joseph and Potiphar's wife. It opens with Joseph enjoying good success because "the LORD was with him." Although he ends up in jail, even there he prospers because "the LORD was with him." In between, he proves himself worthy of greatness because he knew how to say no.

As we wrap up this chapter, I'd like to repeat three points I made in the beginning.

1. Temptation comes to all of us eventually.
2. Temptation itself is not a sin.
3. How you respond makes all the difference.

God is faithful to us when we are tempted. In the moment of temptation, we must be faithful to him. Here are four "don'ts" that will help you think clearly about your own personal struggles:

1. Don't be surprised when temptation knocks at your door.
2. Don't be deceived by persuasive voices.
3. Don't be gentle with your emotions.
4. Don't be confused by the immediate results.

Three Simple Words

If we are going to be victorious over temptation, we must do what Joseph did when Potiphar's wife attempted to seduce him: just say no.

When you are tempted to do wrong this week, just say no.

When someone says, "Come sleep with me," take a deep breath, leave your coat behind, run the other way, and just say no.

When Satan whispers in your ear, "Go on. Everyone else is doing it," remember, everyone else isn't doing it, and just say no.

When you feel like giving someone a piece of your mind, remember that you don't have a piece to spare, so grin and bear it, and just say no.

When a friend says, "You want to hear a good joke?" and you know the joke will do you no good, look him straight in the eye and just say no.

When the boss asks you to sign a report and you know the numbers on it aren't right, remember who you are, smile at him, and just say no.

When your mind plays tricks on you and says, "Go ahead. No one will see you," remember that God sees everything you do, and then just say no.

When it's 5:30 P.M. and the kids are cranky and your husband isn't home yet, and supper isn't ready and the house is filled with dirty socks and dirty diapers, before you reach for the nearest sharp instrument, take a deep breath, look to heaven, count your blessings instead of your problems, and just say no.

When you go to your twentieth high school reunion and you are tempted to keep quiet about your Christian faith when you run into some old friends, just say no to your fears and say yes to your faith.

When you find yourself down and out, up against the wall and under the pile, when nothing is going right and you are hopelessly entangled and you see no way out of the mess you are in, before you say something you shouldn't say or do something you shouldn't do, before you blow your top or give up the ghost, remember that God still loves you and then just say no.

Do You Know Who You Are?

In the end I believe the key to resisting temptation lies in knowing who you are and whose you are. Christian, do you know that you belong to God? His name is tattooed on your soul and written on your heart. You belong to him. If that matters at all to you, it ought to make a difference when you hear the seductive voice of temptation.

Romans 12:1 tells us to present our bodies to God as living sacrifices. Why does God say to present your body? Why doesn't he say to present your soul or your spirit? The answer is simple. If God has your body, he's got you. If you ever decide that your body belongs to God, you'll find it much easier to say no when the devil comes knocking at your door.

Have you ever presented the parts of your body to God?

- Lord, here are my hands.
- Lord, here are my lips.
- Lord, here are my eyes.
- Lord, here are my ears.
- Lord, here are my feet.
- Lord, here is my heart.
- Lord, here is my mind.
- Lord, here are my most private parts.

If you ever decide to get that specific with God, you'll find a level of joy and freedom in Christ you never knew before.

Remember that the Holy Spirit lives within you. If Jesus were visibly beside us, how would we act? What would we say? What would we watch? Where would we not go? The problem is that he is not visibly with us, so we feel free to do what we want without restraint. But we need to realize that the Holy Spirit is inside us, indwelling us. We are his home, his temple (1 Cor. 6:19–20). So wherever we go, we are taking him along with us; what we watch, we watch through the eyes of his dwelling place; what we say issues from his home; when we are rude and obnoxious, he is suffering the indignity of such action coming from where he lives.

There is one final thought that will help us in the hour of temptation. Hebrews 12:2 tells us to "fix our eyes on Jesus." Take a long look at the Son of God who struggled in the wilderness and won the victory over the devil. If he won the battle, so can we because his divine power is available to us today.

Temptation is the common experience of the people of God. We will never escape it as long as we live in a fallen world. But God has given us everything we need to win the battle every time.

Stand and fight, child of God. The Lord is on your side.

A Truth to Remember:
You can overcome temptation if you know who you are and whose you are.

Going Deeper

1. Do you agree that it is not a sin to be tempted? In what sense can temptation be a tool God uses to develop spiritual maturity in us?

2. One paragraph on pages 93–94 lists a number of the "ordinary" temptations we may face every day. Using that list as a starting point, make a list of the temptations that you face on a regular basis. Which ones give you the most trouble?

3. Why is it important we take the "way of escape" the first time it is offered? What harm comes from giving in to "little" sins?

4. Why does God often allow temptation and blessing to come at the same time? Can you think of a time that happened in your own life? How did you respond?

5. "Don't be gentle with your emotions." What does that mean and why is it so important in dealing with our temptations?
6. What one thing sticks in your mind as something you'll want to remember the next time you are tempted?

Taking Action

Using Romans 12:1 as a guide, present the various parts of your body to God. As you do, name some of the temptations that might be associated with your hands, your feet, your stomach, your eyes, your lips, your private parts, and so on. Ask the Lord to give you strength to say no the next time you face each particular temptation.

Chapter 8

IF GOD IS GOOD, WHY DO I HURT?

O f all the questions that trouble the people of God, none is greater than the question posed in the title of this chapter. Sometimes it is asked in other ways: Why is there so much suffering in the world? Or why do bad things happen to good people? Or why do the wicked prosper while the righteous take such a beating? Or if God really has the power to stop human suffering, why doesn't he use it?

Eventually these questions become very personal: Why did my husband leave me after fifteen years? Why did God allow my daughter to die in a car wreck? If God is good, how could he let my closest friend suddenly have a heart attack? There is no end to the questions, and there is an alarming shortage of satisfying answers. No question for a pastor is harder to answer than, "Why did this happen?" Twenty-seven years ago my father died after a short illness. Two years ago one of my best friends died while exercising. Those two events are the most traumatic experiences of my life. As I ponder the question "Why did this happen?" I realize that I don't really know anything more today about why my father died than I knew twenty-seven years ago. God has his reasons, but they are far beyond my meager understanding. The same is true of the death of my dear friend two years ago. Looking around, I can see many lives that have been touched because of his untimely death. Undoubtedly there will be people in heaven who came to Christ as a result of the way he lived and died. But is that the full explanation for why things happened the way they did?

The answer almost certainly is no. I rest content that at best I can grasp a tiny sliver of God's eternal purposes as they work themselves out in a fallen world where death still reigns.

Some people have trouble dealing with unanswerable questions. But as I grow a bit older, I find myself taking comfort in how little I know about how the universe works. In the sad, sorrow-filled days after my friend died, I had a long conversation with the Lord. "So you think I made a mistake by taking Gary home to heaven?" the Lord seemed to say to me. "Yes, I think you made a mistake," I replied. The Lord didn't seem offended by that. He already knew how I felt about it. "So you think I should have asked your opinion before I made my decision?" "Yes, Lord, that's exactly how I feel, and frankly, I wouldn't have made that decision at all. I would have told you to go find someone else to take home to heaven."

Again the Lord didn't seem bothered by my comments. "Ray, just keep this in mind: I did what I did for my own reasons. But I did it without consulting you so you would know that I take full responsibility for when and how Gary died." That conversation, which was all in my mind yet seemed very real to me, was a great comfort to my soul. I find it easy to worship a God who can suddenly and without warning take home a mighty Christian like Gary Olson. I felt then and feel now that only an Almighty God would do something like that and feel no need to explain himself before or after.

In a sense, the mystery of it all ended up building my faith. After all, why would I want to worship a God I could fully understand? "How unsearchable his judgments, and his paths beyond tracing out!" (Rom. 11:33).

And why am I alive while someone else suddenly dies? I faced that question several years ago when the pastor of a large church in Chicago died suddenly. I pastor Calvary Memorial Church; he was the pastor of Calvary Church in another Chicago suburb. I had met him several times and respected him as a man of God. When I heard that he had died, I recalled those words of Scripture, "You sweep men away in the sleep of death; they are like the new grass of the morning—though in the morning it springs up new, by evening it is dry and withered" (Ps. 90:5–6).

The next day someone told me that he had heard the pastor's death announced on a local radio station, but he only heard the part where the announcer said that the pastor of Calvary Church had died suddenly. He assumed they were talking about me. And the thought comes—*It could have been me.* Why the other pastor and not me? I don't know the answer to that question.

The question before us focuses on the connection between God's goodness and our pain. In thinking about where to turn in the Bible to find help on this topic, my mind was drawn to a simple statement in the Book of Job where the afflicted saint declares his faith in God. His words have endured across the centuries because they speak for everyone who has spent some time in the furnace of suffering. Some people are in the furnace right now, others have just come out, and the rest of us will be there sooner or later.

Five Truths for Those in the Furnace

Here is Job's simple statement that sums up an enormous amount of spiritual truth: "He knows the way that I take; when he has tested me, I will come forth as gold" (Job 23:10). From this verse (and the three following verses) I would call your attention to five important truths that if properly understood will help you hang on to your faith while living in the furnace.

Truth #1: God Sees You Even Though You May Not Be Able to See Him

Job begins by affirming his confidence that God sees him in his pain: "He knows the way that I take." It is not an uncommon experience for believers to lose the conscious sense of God's presence during the darkest moments of life. We wonder where God is when we are walking through the pain of divorce, or the crushing burden of having our friends turn on us, or the heartbreak of watching a loved one die. Even the Lord Jesus cried out from the cross, "My God, my God, why have you forsaken me?" (Mark 15:34).

It's not wrong to feel that way, and you have not sinned just because you have lost the sense of God's presence. Job said, "I've got a case to present to the Lord if only I could find him. I've looked high and low for God but I can't find him anywhere. I've searched in every direction but he is nowhere to be found." Then he rose to a higher level of faith and declared, "I can't see him, but it doesn't matter because I know he sees me."

Someone said it this way: "God's hand is invisible but he has an all-seeing eye." Do you recall the story of Hagar, who fled from the household of Abraham and Sarah? Pregnant and alone, she wandered in the barren desert. The Lord found her near a spring and told her to go back to Abraham and Sarah. He also told her to name her son Ishmael, which means "God hears," because the Lord had heard of her misery. She replied with one of the wonderful statements of the Old Testament, "You are the God who sees me" (Gen. 16:13). She actually gave God a name—El Roi—which means in Hebrew, "the God who sees."

Here is a name of God for those going through trials—El Roi—the God who sees. You may not see him but he sees you. He knows what you are going through.

Truth #2: Spiritual Growth Is a Journey, Not a Destination

Notice how Job puts it—"When *he* has tested me." I've italicized the word *he* to emphasize that Job understood that God was behind his sufferings. You may say that it was all Satan's doing, but that's not the whole truth. It was God who brought up Job's name in the first place when he asked, "Have you considered my servant Job?" (Job 1:8). And it was God who set the limits on how far Satan could go in tormenting Job. That's why Job kept saying, "I want to talk to God face to face about all this." Satan may have started it, but God set the rules of the game.

"When he has *tested* me." This speaks to the fact that suffering is part of God's process to bring us to spiritual maturity. Write it down in big letters: We all have to do some furnace time sooner or later. You say, "But it's hot in there." You're right about that. "It hurts." It sure does. "It seems to last forever." That's definitely how it feels inside the furnace. "I don't like it in there." Neither do I. But none of those objections matter in the end.

What is God trying to do when he allows his children to go through hard trials and deep suffering? There are several answers to that question. First, God is purging us of sin and purifying us of iniquity. Second, God uses suffering to test our faith. Will you still obey God in the darkness? Will you serve God when things aren't going your way? Will you hold on to the truth when you feel like giving up? Third, God uses times of difficulty to humble us. When things are going well, we tend to get puffed up about our accomplishments. But let the darkness fall and we are on our knees crying out to God. Fourth, God definitely uses hard times to prepare us to minister to others. He comforts us so that we may comfort others. I know many Christians whose greatest ministry has come from sharing with others how God helped them through a time of crisis. Fifth, I believe God uses hard times to prepare us for a new understanding of his character. In the furnace we discover God's goodness in a way we never experienced it before.

Someone wrote me a note and described several traumatic events of the last two years—including the death of a parent and a very painful divorce. He said that he was glad to see a new year begin because the last one had been filled with so much pain. The whole year he had been living on the brink. But that's not bad, he said, because out on the brink of life he discovered the grace of God. "I have learned I am a person desperately in need of grace," he added. Hard times are a gift from God to help him see how much he needs the Lord. His pain has taught him that he is like a helpless baby, totally dependent on the Lord.

On one level we all know that's true. It's just that we forget it until life falls apart.

Truth #3: Your Trials Will Not Last Forever

The text says, "I will come forth as gold." Looking back from our position, we may not see how great a statement of faith this really is. Job had lost everything—his property, his prosperity, his position in the community, his children, and his health. His wife turned against him when she encouraged him to curse God and die. Here is this man sitting on an ash heap, scraping his sores with pieces of broken pottery. He is a broken and ruined man. Yet in the midst of his pain he declares, "I will come forth as gold."

How can this be? He saw something his three friends didn't see. He understood with the eyes of faith that what God was doing had a purpose. All these terrible things were not meant to destroy him, but in the end to improve him.

We may rightly wonder how tragedy can improve a person. This week I read a book of Puritan prayers. There I found the statement that our trials are sent by God for our spiritual improvement. For some reason that struck me with great force. When God wants to improve a person spiritually, he puts him through great trials.

Job compared it to the process of refining gold. Even though this took place thousands of years ago, the basic process has hardly changed. You take raw chunks of gold ore—pieces of stone flecked with tiny bits of gold—and put them in a hot furnace. The heat causes the stone and dirt to melt and rise to the surface where they are skimmed off so the only thing left is pure gold. It takes enormous heat to do this, but it's worth it because in the end you have pure gold, unmixed with any impurities.

Something like that is at work in your life through the trials you endure. The hotter the fire, the more the pain, but the quicker the gold comes forth. In the end you will be both *approved* and *improved* by God. Your trials are not wasted nor are they random acts of fate.

- You will be *approved*—found to be good.
- You will be *improved*—made to be better.

This may not seem very comforting when you are inside the furnace. If that's where you are right now, little that I can say will help you. Even to promise that it won't last forever may seem empty when the flames are leaping around you. I can't tell you when your trials will end, but I do know this much: He's an on-time God. You can't rush him, but he's never late either. When the appointed time has come, the fierce heat will dissipate and the gold of tested character will come forth in your life.

But what about those people whose trials never end in this life? I must admit that I have known some very fine people whose lives have seemed to be one heartbreak after another. When I see such a person, I never think, "They must be very sinful." Instead I think to myself, "There must be a lot of gold there."

Here's another piece of good news. For those who know Jesus Christ, death is the end of all suffering. This week I ran across a marvelous statement of this truth: "God has an eternity to set right what has gone wrong." That's why the apostle Paul could say that our trials aren't worthy to be compared to the glory that will be revealed in us (Rom. 8:18). Whether you live or die, if you are a Christian, your trials will not last forever.

Truth #4: Faith Is a Conscious Choice to Obey God in Spite of Your Circumstances

Job states his case: "My feet have closely followed his steps; I have kept to his way without turning aside. I have not departed from the commands of his lips; I have treasured the words of his mouth more than my daily bread" (Job 23:11–12).

Here is a man in dire straits—in worse shape than most of us will ever be—and in the midst of his pain he makes a bold declaration: "I'm still serving the Lord. As bad as it's been, nothing can cause me to turn away from God." I ask one simple question: Where does that kind of faith come from? To me that's a crucial question because as I study my own heart, I'm not so sure that I would be as strong as Job under those circumstances. How does a person stay strong when life tumbles in around him? After some years of thinking about this, I have concluded that the people who survive great trials understand that faith is a conscious moment-by-moment choice. More specifically, they also understand that faith is not based on how you feel at any given moment.

For years I tended to view faith as an emotion—if I felt good, if things were going well, if I found myself in a great worship service, then faith was easy for me. There's only one problem with that concept—it won't work when you don't feel good or things aren't going well or your friends have turned against you or the preacher is boring. Feeling-based faith won't cut it when life crashes in on every side.

In those moments of desperation you've got a choice to make. It's exactly the same one Job made. He said, "My feet have followed his steps" and "I have not turned aside." I'm sure Job didn't feel like following God after all the tragedies he had endured. But he did it anyway. That's why he survived—and that's why we still talk about him today.

While doing a radio interview I was asked how I could be so positive and confident when I spoke about God's will. The man asking the question seemed burdened with many cares and difficulties. My answer went this way: "When my father died many years ago, I came face to face with the ultimate unanswerable question of life. I didn't know then why such a good man would have to die at the age of fifty-six or why he would leave my mother and her four sons without a husband and a father. I had no clue about what God was doing. In the years since then I have learned many things about life, but I confess that I still don't understand why my father died. It doesn't make any more sense to me now than it did then. I am older and wiser, but in the one question that really matters I have no answers.

"But I have learned since then that faith is a choice you make. Sometimes you choose to believe because of what you see; often you believe in spite of what you can see. As I look to the world around me, many things remain mysterious and unanswerable. But if there is no God, or if he is not good, then nothing at all makes sense. I have chosen to believe because I must believe. I truly have no other choice. If I sound confident, it is only because I have learned through my tears that my only confidence is in God and God alone."

My older brother Andy is a urologist who lost a twenty-year-old patient to a rare form of kidney cancer. When he asked me in all seriousness, "Why did he die?" I had no answer. But I felt no shame in saying that. I have decided to believe that God is good and can be trusted no matter what happens. If I didn't believe that, I wouldn't have the strength to get out of bed every day.

I received an E-mail from one of the senior adults in my congregation who has been battling cancer for several years. The doctors told her they have done all they could, which means that every day from here on out is what you might call bonus time. More than once she has been on the brink of death only to pull back from the edge. Through all of it her faith has been strong and even radiant. This is how she put it in her message to me: "Not sure how many more treatments there will be, but whatever the Lord has in store, so be it. He is in control at all times and has always been. God is indeed a loving God." That's not the testimony of a person dying of cancer. It's the testimony of a child of God living by faith.

I have a lifelong friend in Alabama who has been battling cancer for several years. Right now the cancer is in remission, but the doctors have said that the cancer could return again. Many people have prayed for his complete healing. When I chatted with him on the phone, he said that he'd been pondering his own situation from a new perspective. Which is the greater miracle, he wondered, to be healed from cancer or to be given the grace to stay faithful even if he isn't healed completely?

Faith comes in many different varieties, but the faith that wins in the end is faith that chooses to obey God in spite of the outward circumstances.

Truth #5: God Is God and He Has the Absolute Right to Do Whatever He Wishes

There is one final secret of Job's steadfast faith. In Job 23:13 he declares concerning the Lord, "But he stands alone, and who can oppose him? He does whatever he pleases." That brings us once again to the First Rule of the Spiritual Life: He's God and we're not. Until we understand that, we're going to be unhappy because we'll end up fighting against God.

Several years ago I read the biography of Bob Pierce, who founded World Vision, the Christian relief organization that has helped millions of people around the world.[12] As I read his story, it struck me that he was an unlikely man to found and lead such a large organization. He didn't have much education, he butchered the "King's English," and he lacked many social graces. In fact, he called himself a second-rater. When asked the secret of his life, he said that in his early years as a Christian he had prayed, "O God, I give you the right to set the agenda for my life. From here on out, you're going to run the show. And you can change that agenda any time you want. But I pray that you will be pleased to use me for your glory in any way you see fit. Amen."

That's the kind of prayer God can answer because it's based on the truth that God is God and he has the absolute right to do whatever he wants. Many of us are unhappy because we're fighting God at the point of his sovereignty. We've never surrendered our agenda to his control.

To borrow a common phrase, we must "let God be God." On one level that statement is nonsense because God is God whether we like it or not. But on another level it points to a great truth. We can either live in submission to the sovereignty of a God whose ways are far beyond all human understanding or we can attempt to fight against his plan. But as the wise man said: Your arms are too short to box with God.

What should you do when you find yourself in the furnace?

- Seek a quiet heart.
- Listen for God's voice.
- Look for God's fingerprints.
- Stay faithful to God no matter what.

Above all, don't take matters into your own hands. That only makes things worse. God has wonderful things to teach you in the furnace if only you will listen and learn. We'll all do some furnace time because that's part of God's plan for our spiritual growth. You can't escape the furnace, but you can use it for your own spiritual improvement.

Back to the Original Question

And that brings me back to the original question: If God is good, why do I hurt? I think the first part of that question is the key. Is God really good? More and more I am convinced that this is the fundamental question of life: "Is God good and can he be trusted to do what is right?" If the answer is yes, then we can face the worst that life has to offer. If the answer is no, then we're no better off than the people who have no faith at all. In fact, if the answer is no or if we're not sure, then we really don't have any faith at all.

Sometimes you choose to believe because of what you see; often you believe in spite of what you can see. As I look at the world around me, many things remain mysterious and unanswerable. But if there is no God, or if he is not good, then nothing at all makes sense.

When we hurt, we really have only two choices:

- we can hurt with God, or
- we can hurt without him.

If you are hurting as you read these words, you may feel as if you have come to the end of your endurance. I pray that you will hang on to the Lord. If you turn away from him, things can only get worse.

Pioneer missionary J. Hudson Taylor founded the China Inland Mission one hundred years ago. During the terrible days of the Boxer Rebellion, when missionaries were being captured and killed, he went through such an agony of soul that he could not pray. Writing in his journal, he summarized his spiritual condition this way: "I can't read. I can't think. I can't pray. But I can trust."

There will be times when we can't read the Bible. Sometimes we won't be able to focus our thoughts on God at all. Often we will not even be able to pray. But in those moments when we can't do anything else, we can still trust in the loving purposes of our heavenly Father.

Fear not, child of God. No one knows what a day may bring. Who knows if we will make it through this week? But our God is faithful to keep every one of his promises. Nothing can happen to us that does not first pass through the hands of a loving God. If your way is dark, hang on to Jesus. When your furnace time is over, you will come forth as gold.

A Truth to Remember:
God has wonderful things to teach you in the furnace if only you will listen and learn.

Going Deeper

1. Do you agree that every Christian has to do some "furnace time" sooner or later? Why does God allow hard times to come to his children?

2. Think back to a time when you did some "furnace time." How long were you in the furnace? What did you learn from it? What "gold" was produced in your life?

3. As you look back on your "furnace time" experiences, how were you helped (or hurt) by what other Christians did or said? Name some things we can do when we see a brother or sister in Christ going through a hard time.

4. What difference does it make to someone dying of cancer to know that "our suffering is temporary"? Is it a cop-out to say such a thing since suffering for some people won't end until they get to heaven? How can this truth give hope in a situation that humanly speaking seems hopeless?

5. How do our sufferings "qualify" us to minister to others?

6. In what area of your life do you need to "let God be God"? What do you need to do (or stop doing) to make sure that happens?

Taking Action

Take another look at the prayer of Bob Pierce: "O God, I give you the right to set the agenda for my life. From here on out, you're going to run the show. And you can change that agenda any time you want. But I pray that you will be pleased to use me for your glory in any way you see fit. Amen." The challenge is simple. Write this prayer on a piece of paper, place it where you can see it every day, and pray it at least once a day for the next week. Then get ready to be surprised as God begins to work his agenda in your life.

Chapter 9

WHAT IS SPIRITUAL WARFARE?

"Can the devil come to church?" The young man who asked me that question was both sincere and intense. He had heard a television preacher say that the devil comes to church all the time. How do you answer a question like that? As I thought about it later, two comments came to mind. First, I am sure that the devil feels right at home in some churches, especially those that no longer believe the Bible or preach the gospel. Second, the people in those churches would probably laugh at the question and also at my answer. Many people today doubt the existence of a personal being called the devil. That there is evil in the world, they readily admit. Who could deny it? But in the minds of many, that evil stems from a bad environment, a flawed home life, or perhaps a lack of good education. If only we could change our circumstances, we could change human nature. Or so we are told.

But thousands of years of human history point to a different answer. Evil is in the world because evil is in us. When the *London Times* asked various leaders to explain what was wrong with the world, G. K. Chesterton offered a terse reply: "What is wrong with the world? I am." His answer was entirely biblical. Something has gone wrong with the world because something has gone wrong with us. And that something is called sin. All of us feel it, know it, and if we are honest, we confess that sin is not simply "out there"; it is also deeply embedded in who we are.

If we are willing to admit the truth about ourselves (that we are sinners), it should not be difficult to admit that there is indeed a malevolent being called the devil who actively makes war against us. And since the devil is a spirit being, that means he can go wherever we go, including to church with us.

Spiritual warfare begins with the observation that we are in a battle against the world, the flesh, and the devil. All believers instinctively realize that they are called to fight—to be good soldiers, to put on their armor, to take up the weapons of righteousness, to enter the fray unafraid, to stand against the fierce assault of evil, and having done all, to stand victorious at the end of the day.

Here are a few questions that come to mind as we begin our discussion:

- What is spiritual warfare and how should we engage in it?
- What part does Satan play in this great drama?
- How do we fight so that we might win?
- In what sense is Satan already defeated?
- What role do demons play in spiritual warfare?
- What is warfare praying and why is it important?
- How much influence can Satan have over me if I am a genuine believer?
- Will there be any end to spiritual warfare in this life?
- What is the "armor of God" and how do I put it on?

Before we deal with those questions, let's pause to consider why the topic of spiritual warfare has become so popular in our day. One obvious reason stems from a new interest in the occult in Western thinking. The last thirty years have seen an unprecedented openness to witchcraft, channeling, reincarnation, and all sorts of paranormal experiences. The rise of spiritual warfare teaching is a natural response to this trend. This new openness to the supernatural stems from the collapse of Enlightenment rationalism and the entrance of postmodernism. For several centuries science was thought to have the answer for everything, including the realm once reserved for theology. Today the notion of truth as an absolute concept has nearly disappeared. This has opened the door to a new emphasis on various kinds of supernatural experiences.

The contemporary interest in the occult illustrates the spiritual starvation of this generation. Because God has put eternity inside every heart (Eccl. 3:11), we are all born with a desire to understand the world around us. We want to know who we are, where we come from, who made us, why we are here, and what the universe is all about. We can seek those answers in the Bible and discover the truth, or we can turn to mediums, witches, and wizards and discover another completely different set of answers. If we don't fill the "God-shared vacuum" inside the heart with God himself, we will fill it with the spiritual junk food we find all around us.

For many people personal experience is the arbiter of all truth claims. Recently I had an exchange on an Internet discussion board with a young man who defended a particular religious activity by saying, "I cannot deny my own experience." This evidently is meant to trump any arguments based on Scripture. But the experience orientation (which isn't altogether bad) has opened up a whole generation to certain practices that may not be spiritually healthy.

Popular Christian fiction has made spiritual warfare accessible to millions of readers. While on the one hand we can be thankful that many people have awakened to the contemporary reality of angels and demons, there is also reason to be concerned that some people have lost their spiritual balance and have focused on the demonic in a way that is not productive for spiritual growth.

A Place to Begin

Here are a few statements that will help us think biblically about spiritual warfare.

Satan is a real being and the demons who follow him are also real. Satan is a fallen angel and the demons are fallen angels who are in perpetual rebellion against God. The demons are spirit-beings whose only purpose is to further Satan's evil purposes in the world (Matt. 12:24; 1 Tim. 4:1–2; Eph. 6:12). Satan and the demons are active in the world today, and their activity will increase as we near the end of the age (Rev. 12:9–12).

The Bible tells us just enough to pique our curiosity but not enough to answer all our questions. Imagine yourself at a play in a majestic theater. As you wait for the program to begin, you can hear noise from behind the curtain, and occasionally the curtain itself is jostled by something or someone hidden from your view. Suddenly the curtain opens for a moment, just for a second, and you can clearly see the action on the stage. Almost before you can focus your eyes, the curtain closes again. You know what you saw, but you wish you had been able to get a better glimpse. In numerous biblical passages we are allowed to peek behind the curtain of history to see things that are normally invisible.

It is easy to go to extremes in this area. On one hand, you can give Satan too much credit and build your Christian life around what Satan is doing. Or you can ignore Satan, pay no attention to his schemes, and fall into his clutches through carelessness.

The only things we know with certainty about spiritual warfare are the things revealed in the Bible. Some well-known Christian leaders have written extensive descriptions about the spirit world that come not from the Bible but from personal counseling experience. The danger is that we may unconsciously elevate what someone said in a counseling session to a level equal with the Bible. And we may even make spiritual decisions on things allegedly said by demons speaking through troubled individuals. That road leads eventually to spiritual confusion. Experience may *illustrate* biblical truth; it cannot *replace* it. Furthermore, experience must not be used to "fill in the blanks" in areas where the Scripture is silent.

Spiritual warfare rightly understood is not a minor biblical topic. In some ways it might be termed the whole story of the Bible. The conflict between God and Satan started in heaven when Lucifer rebelled, came to earth when Adam and Eve sinned, and continues in every generation in the ongoing struggle between good and evil. That conflict will not end until the devil is finally cast into the lake of fire and the New Jerusalem comes down out of heaven (Rev. 20–22).

Spiritual warfare is the ongoing battle between the believer and the devil. The devil uses the power of the flesh and the allure of the world to cause us to turn away from God. His ultimate goal is the capture and destruction of every human being. This explains why the Christian life is a battleground, not a playground.

Some Myths about Spiritual Warfare

Because spiritual warfare is controversial, it is important that we deal briefly with three popular but wrong ideas.

Myth #1: Spiritual Warfare Is Unreal, Unbiblical, and Unhistorical

This is the viewpoint of liberalism and anti-supernaturalism. Some people simply don't believe in the existence of a personal devil. For them the whole subject of spiritual warfare is something like a medieval fairy tale. Sometimes untaught believers share this viewpoint.

Against it we have the whole testimony of holy Scripture. From beginning to end the Bible testifies to the reality of a personal being called the devil and Satan who is the enemy of God, the opponent of God's people, a liar from the beginning, and a roaring lion who would destroy us if he could (1 Pet. 5:8).

We also have the testimony of the saints of God of every age. During the Puritan era a man named William Gurnall published a thick book called *The Christian in Complete Armor*. His subtitle tells the whole story: "The saints' war against the devil, wherein a discovery is made of that grand enemy of God and his people, in his policies, power, seat of his empire, wickedness, and chief design he hath against the saints; a magazine opened, from when the Christian is furnished with spiritual arms for the battle, helped on with his armor, and taught use of his weapons; together with the happy issue of the whole war." That does seem to cover the whole topic!

This battle between the saints and Satan is as old as the Garden of Eden. It is also a part of every believer's life.

Myth #2: Spiritual Warfare Must Be Carried On by Professionals or It Requires Special Training

The Bible says nothing about a special class of "spiritual warfare experts" who are trained in confronting demons, casting them out, and so on. Some people even believe there is a "gift" of spiritual warfare. If there is, the Bible says nothing about it. The biblical emphasis is always on the responsibility of every believer. All believers are to put on the armor of God (Eph. 6:10–17). All believers are told to be good soldiers of the gospel (2 Tim. 2:3–4). All believers are warned to be on the alert against Satan (James 4:7). The danger of this myth is that we may end up with a "priestcraft" of spiritual warriors who are exalted above the rest of the body of Christ.

Myth #3: Spiritual Warfare Necessarily Involves Spectacular Confrontations with the Devil and His Demons

This appears to be the view of some contemporary leaders who speak of "power encounters" with the devil. Some even cast out demons publicly and with great fanfare. Into this whole category would go such things as exorcisms, deliverance meetings, and so on.

In mentioning these things I do not wish to question the motives of those leaders. Only God can judge the human heart. However, a confrontational mentality often seems to develop. Some even talk about hand-to-hand combat, wrestling with the demons, sensing, seeing, naming, rebuking the demons one by one, and striking them down with dramatic words of authority. Whatever truth may lie in this direction, it can also lead to spiritual pride because we may end up thinking we control the spirit world. Our pride may open us to unwitting spiritual disaster.

How God Uses Satan to Accomplish His Purposes

In thinking about spiritual warfare, it's crucial that we base our beliefs on good theology. That is, we need to make sure that what we do and say in this area corresponds with what the Bible actually teaches. Some Christians attribute more power to Satan than he possesses. Although the precise details of Satan's fall are shrouded in mystery, this much is certain: He was always only a created being whom God allowed to rebel. That statement is all-important because some people have exalted the devil to a position where he is "almost-but-not-quite-God." They attribute so much power to him that he becomes in their minds a "junior God" who can do almost everything God can do. But the Bible teaches no such thing. Although mighty in power when compared to humans, Satan is nothing at all when compared to God. The Bible never presents him as omnipotent, omnipresent, or omniscient.

This raises a question that is difficult to answer precisely. How much power does Satan have? Clearly he is the most powerful of all the created angels (Isa. 14:12–15). He came to Eve as a serpent (Gen. 3:1). In Revelation he appears as a fierce dragon (Rev. 12). Peter calls him a "roaring lion" (1 Pet. 5:8). Paul says he masquerades as an "angel of light" (2 Cor. 11:14). The Lord Jesus called him the "father of lies" and a "murderer from the beginning" (John 8:44). He is also called the "prince of this world" (John 12:31), the "god of this age" (2 Cor. 4:4), the "ruler of the kingdom of the air" (Eph. 2:2), and the "accuser of our brothers" (Rev. 12:10). Obviously he is a created being with powers that are supernatural and go far beyond what any human possesses.

But we must not exaggerate his power either. Satan has exactly as much power as God permits him to have—not one iota more. As Martin Luther said, the devil is "God's devil," meaning that God puts limits on what he can do. For instance, when Satan wanted to cause Job to curse God, God told Satan he could touch him physically but he could not take Job's life. Likewise, Jesus said that Satan had asked to "sift" Peter (Luke 22:31), meaning that he had to ask God's permission before tempting Peter to deny Christ. This raises many questions about the relationship between God's permission to Satan and the temptations we face every day. Two things should be very clear to every Christian. First, Satan serves God's purposes in ways we cannot fully understand. Second, when we are tempted, we must not blame Satan for our weakness. We are fully responsible for the moral choices we make.

William Gurnall states the truth about Satan in colorful language that may seem shocking to our ears: "When God says 'Stay!' he must stand like a dog by the table while the saints feast on God's comfort. He does not dare to snatch even a tidbit, for the Master's eye is always upon him." This simply means that Satan, as powerful as he is, is not autonomous. He has no independent power of his own. Like any other created being, he must submit to God's control.

This leads to a further question. Why is it important to see Satan in his proper biblical light? There are several clear answers to that question. First, so that we might worship God as the supreme Lord of the universe. Second, so that we will have the courage to stand against the devil and his attacks against us. Third, so that we will not give the devil more credit that he deserves. Good theology and spiritual victory always go hand in hand. We should respect the devil's power and not take him lightly, but we should not live in cringing fear of what he might do to us. If we live in fear, we are defeated before the battle begins.

One final question and we can move on. If the devil is always subject to God, why is he alive and apparently doing so well today? Why hasn't God destroyed him yet? We must say with great reverence that we can't answer this question completely. The secret things belong to the Lord our God (Deut. 29:29). But this much we can say with certainty: In some way that is not fully understandable to our finite minds, Satan serves God's purposes in the world today. Certainly this comes as a result of creating men and women with the ability to make uncoerced moral choices. Perhaps in a world where we can choose to do wrong, a being like the devil must exist. When God's purposes have been fully served, the devil will be cast in the lake of fire where he will remain in perpetual torment for all eternity (Rev. 20:10).

On a personal note, I have found it helpful, when facing what seems to be an onslaught of evil and spiritual confusion, to paraphrase the words of Joseph: "Satan means it for evil but God means it for good." With that perspective even in the worst moments, we may see God's hand at work.

Practical Steps in Resisting Satanic Attack

In 2 Corinthians 2:11, Paul comments that we are not unaware of Satan's schemes. He comes to us in many different ways and in many different guises. Some days he may reason with us as he did with Eve in the Garden of Eden. Other times he will suggest evil thoughts that fill our minds with anger, bitterness, hatred, lust, and greed. He also works through false teachers to promote false doctrine in the church. In those cases he may first seem like an "angel of light." But he always reveals his true colors sooner or later. We know he attempts to seduce believers through pornography, sexual immorality of all types, drug and alcohol abuse, and through any involvement in the occult. Above all, remember that Satan does not warn before he strikes. That is why we must constantly be on our guard.

How should we respond to Satan's attacks on us? Martin Luther said that when the devil comes knocking at the door, just send the Lord Jesus to answer it. Here are some practical ways to do that.

Cry out to God for help. This may seem elementary, but it is not. One part of resisting the devil is to ask God for his help. When we are tempted, we must immediately call out to the Lord and confess our weakness. The precise words don't matter so much as the attitude of our heart. If we think we can defeat Satan on our own, we will soon learn the truth the hard way. When we confess that we are helpless and will soon be defeated, the Lord will rush to our aid. He loves to help those who call on him.

Don't be discouraged when the battle is hard. The word *resist* is a military term. It means to erect a defense in the face of repeated attacks. But it also contains the idea of swarming over the battlements at the right moment, moving to the offensive, and sweeping the enemy from the field. Just as Satan came to Christ three times, we should not be surprised that he comes to us again and again and again. Sometimes we will face the same temptation hundreds of times over many months or years. And we may struggle with some spiritual issues for a lifetime. Since Satan does not give up easily, we must not think ourselves to be unworthy saints when the battle is fierce. Spiritual warfare lasts until we die. There are many battles, many skirmishes, many foes to face as we march along the highway from earth to heaven.

Take the way of escape the very first time. When faced with temptation, we must take the "way of escape" God provides for us (1 Cor. 10:13). This includes fleeing sinful situations (2 Tim. 2:22), confessing Christ openly (Matt. 10:32; Heb. 10:32; Rev. 12:11), putting to death the deeds of the flesh (Rom. 8:13), yielding our bodies to God (Rom. 6:13), relying on the power of the Holy Spirit (Gal. 5:16), and choosing the path of costly obedience (Luke 9:52). God isn't required to give us a second or third "way of escape" if we have spurned his first one.

Put on the whole armor of God. It would be a useful spiritual exercise to memorize Ephesians 6:10–17. In that passage we are told to "put on" the belt of truth (commitment to integrity and honesty), the breastplate of righteousness (commitment to obeying God in every circumstance), and to have our feet fitted with the gospel of peace (being ready to share the Good News with others). We are to "take up" the shield of faith (choosing to believe God is who he said he is, and acting accordingly), the helmet of salvation (your assurance that you are truly saved by God), and the sword of the Spirit (reading, meditating on, quoting, and believing the written Word of God). Finally, we are to "pray in the Spirit" (v. 18), which means to be in constant communication with God. As we use the armor God has provided, we will find ourselves fully equipped for every battle that may come our way.

Use Scripture the same way Christ did. When Jesus faced the devil after his forty days in the wilderness, he countered the devil's every move with a quotation from Scripture (Matt. 4:1–11). Satan has no answer when the Word of God is used correctly by a believer who is walking in the power of the Spirit. This means we must become people of the Book. We must read it daily, meditate upon it, learn what it says, memorize key verses, and most of all, we must actively stand upon what it says.

Use the resources of the body of Christ. Sometimes Satan wins a battle in our lives because we are ashamed to admit we struggle in a certain area. But it is precisely at this point that we need our brothers and sisters. This is why we have local churches, Sunday school classes, Bible study groups, and accountability partners. The

Christian is a soldier serving in an army, not a guerilla fighting a lonely battle in the jungle. Satan's lures won't seem so attractive when we talk them over with concerned Christian friends. Remember, it's better to ask for prayer when you are tempted than to wish you had.

A Few Controversial Areas

In recent years much discussion about spiritual warfare has focused on such things as territorial spirits, generational demons, naming the demons, casting out demons, and whether or not a true Christian can be demon-possessed. In a book like this it is not possible to discuss these issues in any depth. In all things our theology must be based on what the Bible actually says. We need not and should not go beyond what is revealed in Scripture. It is clear that believers can be harassed in various ways by demons and that we may resist that harassment by the steps I have already suggested. That covers the vast majority of issues most of us are likely to face on a daily basis. Spiritual warfare is less about the details of demonology and much more about our own determination to walk in obedience before the Lord.

Warfare Praying

If you hear someone mention "warfare praying," it's important to remember that this is not a special category of prayer. It simply means that prayer is crucial in our ongoing battle against the devil and all his works. The Lord's Prayer (Matt. 6:9–13) offers a useful model for all our praying. We begin by focusing on God:

- His name—hallowed be your name.
- His kingdom—your kingdom come.
- His will—your will be done.

Then we focus on our own needs:

- Provision—our daily bread.
- Pardon—forgive us our debts.
- Protection—lead us not into temptation.

I take it that "lead us not into temptation, but deliver us from the evil one" means something like "Lord, when I have the desire to sin, may I not have the opportunity. And when I have the opportunity, may I not have the desire. Deliver me from Satan's power because without your deliverance I will fall into his trap every time."

Let the Battle Begin

We can wrap up this chapter with a few concluding comments. It's important to seek a biblical balance in this area. We want to believe everything the Bible says about spiritual warfare, and this means taking the whole Bible into account. We must base our theology on the Bible, not on human experience. We needn't listen to the demons when we have the Word of God as our infallible guide to the truth.

We should expect testing and should not be surprised when it happens. Robert Murry M'Cheyne put it this way: "There can never be peace in the bosom of the believer. There is peace with God, but a constant war with sin." Remember that God allows spiritual warfare as a crucial component of your spiritual growth. Salvation is free, but becoming a disciple of Christ will cost you all that you have. God uses the attacks of Satan to bring us to new personal dependence on the Lord. That's why daily obedience is more important than spectacular experiences. We need not have "power encounters" with the devil or his demons in order to walk in spiritual victory. The most important secret to victory is getting up each day and doing what God has called you to do. That counts for more than talking to the devil or casting out demons.

Finally, rest on this truth: God has given you everything you need to fight and win the battle:

- The Word of God
- The Holy Spirit
- The armor of God
- A new nature
- A new position
- The body of Christ
- The weapon of prayer
- Christ interceding for you in heaven

Martin Luther summed it up well in his great hymn, "A Mighty Fortress Is Our God":

And tho' this world, with devils filled,
Should threaten to undo us,
We will not fear, for God hath willed
His truth to triumph thro' us:
The Prince of Darkness grim,
We tremble not for him;
His rage we can endure,
For lo, his doom is sure,
One little word shall fell him.

That "little word" is Jesus. The cross proved that Jesus is the victor over the devil for time and eternity. We're in a battle whose outcome was determined before the universe began. From our standpoint we smell the smoke of battle and see the flash of musketry as Satan and his hosts move against us. We feel the rumble of the mighty cannon and sense that a huge battle is being waged on every side. Sometimes we stumble and sometimes we fall under the crushing blows of the enemy.

But God says us to us, "Arise, my child. Rise and face your enemy. He is already defeated. Stand and fight in my power and you cannot lose." Let the battle begin.

A Truth to Remember:
God has given you everything you need to fight and win the battle.

Going Deeper

1. How would you define spiritual warfare? Why is this a subject every Christian should know about?
2. Who is Satan and where did he come from? What happens when we exaggerate or underestimate his power?
3. Using the New Testament as your guide, list at least ten different resources Christians can rely on in our struggle against the world, the flesh, and the devil.
4. Think of a time when you consciously resisted the devil in your life. How did you do it? What was the specific circumstance? What was the outcome?
5. Of the six steps for resisting Satan's attacks, which one do you most need to put into practice right now?
6. Why is it dangerous for Christians to dabble in the occult? What harm can come from such things as reading your horoscope or calling a psychic hotline or consulting a fortune-teller? Should Christians be concerned about television shows or movies with heavily occult themes? Why or why not?

Taking Action

Read Ephesians 6:10–17 out loud several times. Then write down each piece of armor and what it might look like in your life. Be very specific—for example, Belt of Truth: "Speaking only the truth when I try to close a sale." Use this as a prayer guide for the next seven days.

Chapter 10

HOW CAN I SHARE
MY FAITH?

Let me describe a situation and ask how you would respond. Let's suppose that you are a missionary arriving for service in a country you have never visited. Although you didn't plan to visit the capital city, your itinerary was changed suddenly and now you find yourself alone in a place filled with people whose education and intelligence equals your own—and in many cases surpasses it. The city is filled with people discussing art and debating philosophy. They love it when someone proposes a new idea because it means they have something to argue about during the hot afternoon hours. People come from many countries to join the ongoing discussion and to admire the many works of art that line the streets.

You are the first Christian ever to visit this world-class city. There are no churches, no Christian bookstores, and no Christian radio stations. You can't find a Christian symbol of any kind in the entire city. You venture further, walking down one street, then another, marveling at the statues and reading the many inscriptions. It is very clear that the people in this city have never heard of Jesus Christ. If you say his name, all you get in return is a blank stare. They know nothing about his birth, his life, his death, his resurrection, or his ascension into heaven.

You are the first Christian in this city and you are the only Christian. No one came before you to prepare the way. No one invited you to come. No one expected your arrival. No one welcomed your appearance. Here you are in the center of the greatest city in the world representing Jesus Christ.

What will you do? Where will you stay? How will you find an opening for the gospel? Let me repeat that you never intended to come to this city, but your plans changed and here you are. The people of this city pride themselves on their intellect, their culture, and their philosophy. No one comes in and teaches them anything. In modern terms, they have "home court advantage."

What will you do now? Where will you begin? How will you find someone to talk to? And who will listen to your message?

- You could hold a tent meeting, but who would come?
- You could show Billy Graham films, but who is Billy Graham to them?
- You could put up a sign advertising a new church, which in this case would be absolutely correct since the new church would also be the first church.
- You could go door-to-door. That's always a good idea, especially if your goal is to listen as least as much as you talk.
- You could rent a meeting room in a local hotel, post some fliers, and invite passersby to attend your services.
- You could pray for some kind of shocking event, such as an earthquake, that would give you a platform to minister to people physically and spiritually.

Or you might decide to take a pass and enjoy a few days of unplanned vacation. After all, you never planned to come here and you don't have any friends who can introduce you to the movers and shakers. And most of all, your coworkers are scattered in other places, so whatever you do, you're going to have to do all alone. To be perfectly honest, many of us would choose the latter course of action. Big cities are hard enough to reach when you have a team. When you are by yourself, they can seem overwhelming.

The World Has Come to the Cities

I live in a suburb of the city of Chicago, but my home is only one-half mile from the city limits. In the village of Oak Park, just over 53,000 people live in an area of 4.5 square miles. We're squeezed together and sometimes it seems as if we're on top of one another. Eight million people live in greater Chicago, which makes it one of the largest cities in America.

Today the world is moving to the cities. As of the year 2000, for the first time in history more than 50 percent of the world's population lives in a city. That's up from just 9 percent in 1900. In 1997 the *New York Times* reported that one New York neighborhood contained people from 123 different countries. That's two-thirds of the nations of the world represented in just one zip code.[13]

What is true of New York is also true of London, Miami, Mexico City, Singapore, New Delhi, and Nairobi. The world is moving to the cities, which means that almost every town is becoming a miniature United Nations. It also means that you don't have to go overseas to encounter the kind of situation I described. All you have to do is go next door or to the next cubicle at work or look to the person seated two rows away in school. The cities, which once were melting pots, have now become stew pots where every imaginable religious point of view can be found.

Jesus said, "Go into all the world and preach the gospel to every creature." For two thousand years Christians have been trying to obey that command. If you combine all the people who call themselves Christians from all the various groups and denominations, the total comes to just under two billion. That sounds good until you consider that there are more than six billion people in the world. And I'm not even going to consider at this point how many of those two billion Christians actually have a genuine personal relationship with Jesus Christ. Even giving ourselves the maximum benefit of the doubt, we've still got two-thirds of the world left to reach.

Before I go any further, let me say plainly that this is not a chapter about becoming a missionary to some distant land. I'm not going to ask you to volunteer to go to Bolivia or Finland or Bangladesh. I have the highest respect for the men and women who volunteer as missionaries, but that's not what this is about.

So what am I talking about? Perhaps an illustration will make things clear. On a recent cable news program, the host read a letter from a viewer complaining that he had said there is no such thing as absolute truth. The viewer wrote to object, pointing out that the Bible is the Word of God and thus the standard for measuring right and wrong. The host smiled and said, "Perhaps it is for you, but not necessarily for everyone else." For the moment, let's not quibble about how the Bible can be the Word of God for one person and not for another. Just focus on the thought itself. The man is obviously well-educated and articulate. He delivered his one-sentence answer as if it were the most obvious truth in the world. His "true for you but not true for me" comment has virtually become the slogan of this generation. My question is this: How do you share Christ with a person who doesn't believe in absolute truth? Thirty years ago educated skeptics loved to argue; today they have a "Big Tent" religion where everyone is partly right and no one is totally wrong.

This chapter is about the challenge of reaching our friends and neighbors with the gospel of Jesus Christ. It begins with the assumption that many people we rub shoulders with every day have little or no knowledge of genuine Christianity. In many cases what little they know has been mixed with strange versions of postmodern pragmatism. They value experience above doctrine and tolerance above truth. They are willing to listen, but they hate to make up their minds.

And that brings me back to the earlier scenario, which in some ways isn't far from the truth. For millions of people today, Christianity simply doesn't figure into their thinking one way or the other. If you were the first Christian to visit a major city, what would you do? Where would you begin?

You should know that I didn't make up this story. What I described is precisely the situation a man named Paul faced when he came alone to the city of Athens. We know he was alone from his comments in 1 Thessalonians 3:1. We know what he did from the record in Acts 17:16–34. Those nineteen verses tell of one of the most dramatic encounters in the history of the Christian faith. Wilbur Smith comments that relatively few men ever change the world. Most men live and die without making even a small ripple, and they leave no trace when they are gone. Not so with Paul. His ministry changed the world forever—and it is still changed twenty centuries later because of what he did in Athens.

A City Full of Idols

Most of us know Athens as the cradle of Western civilization. When we think of Athens, names like Socrates, Plato, Aristotle, Pericles, Sophocles, and Aristophanes come to mind. These are men whose words are still studied in every major university in the world. In Paul's day there were three great universities in the Roman Empire—Tarsus, Alexandria, and the greatest of all in Athens. Here you could find the Academy of Plato, the Lyceum of Aristotle, the Porch of Zeno, and the Garden of Epicurus.

We also connect Athens with Mount Olympus and the pantheon of Greek gods such as Zeus, Athena, and Aphrodite. During the golden age of Pericles, the Athenians built the renowned Parthenon on top of the Acropolis, the massive hill dominating the city. They also built statues in honor of their gods on almost every corner. According to Pliny, there were more than thirty thousand statues in Athens. Petronius says that it was easier to find a god in Athens than a man. Pausanius adds that there were more statues of gods in Athens than in all the rest of Greece.

Most of those were built several hundred years before the New Testament era. By the time Paul arrived some time in the year A.D. 50, Athens was in the late afternoon of its glory. Though Rome was the capital of the empire, Athens was the intellectual and cultural capital of the world.

We pick up the story in Acts 17:16: "While Paul was waiting for them in Athens, he was greatly distressed to see that the city was full of idols." Paul never intended to come to Athens—and certainly not alone. He was waiting for Silas and Timothy to arrive. Since he had some time on his hands, he toured the city, saw its many famous sites, and concluded it was "full of idols." That phrase is actually one word in Greek—an unusual word that means the city was completely given over to idol worship. Eugene Peterson says that Athens was "a junk-yard of idols" (*The Message*). The Athenians would have been shocked by this assessment because they didn't consider these marvelous works of art to be idols. They erected statues in honor of their gods— and to aid in the worship of those gods. To call them idols seems degrading for objects so stunningly beautiful. But Paul wasn't fooled by their outward appearance. He knew an idol when he saw one— and in Athens he saw a city wholly given over to idolatry. Wilbur Smith comments that "a man's character, a man's interest, the pur-poses of a man's life, will determine what he sees, wherever he goes."[14] Some saw works of art; Paul saw idols.

A "Gut" Reaction

What you look for determines what you see; what you see deter-mines what you feel; what you feel determines what you do. Paul had a single eye for the glory of God, and therefore when he saw statues honoring false gods, he wasn't fooled by their beauty; he knew they were idols. Verse 16 tells us he was "greatly distressed." It's a very strong word that describes a deep emotional reaction to the idolatry of Athens. It is a combination of anger and sadness. It's the same word used in the Old Testament to describe God's anger over the sin of his people.

Not long ago I spoke to the Jos-ECWA Theological Seminary in Jos, Nigeria. When I explained the meaning of "greatly distressed," I stepped from behind the pulpit and began to rub my belly in circles. Immediately the students, men and women from across West Africa, began to make a kind of humming noise as they listened. The provost told me later that to speak of deep emotion as coming from the lower abdomen is a very African concept. It means an emotional reaction that goes beyond the head and reaches to the depths of the body. That's what Paul felt when he saw Athens filled with idols.

What does it take to make you angry? Ecclesiastes 3:1 says, "There is a time for everything," which means there is a time for anger. There is a time to be silent and then there is a time to speak out against moral corruption and sinful pride. The men of Athens thought they had built the greatest city on earth—the epitome of pagan humanism. It was if they had erected a sign that read, "Welcome to Athens: City of a Thousand Gods." Paul got angry when he toured Athens. His moral conscience was offended by their pagan idol worship. It didn't matter to him that the Parthenon was one of the wonders of the ancient world or that this was the hometown of Socrates, Plato, and Aristotle. What good was the human mind unless it was offered up in the service of the living God? And why praise the work of men whose architecture exists to honor pagan deities?

A Time for Anger

There are some things that ought to make us angry. We ought to be angry at the legalized killing of the unborn. We ought to be angry about the celebration of homosexuality in our society. We ought to be angry about rampant divorce, deadbeat dads, broken homes, child abuse, spouse abuse, racial prejudice, moral apostasy by so-called Christian leaders, dishonesty in high places, and the brutal treatment of the poor and the homeless. Most of all, we ought to be angry when we see God's name mocked, his Word ignored, and his people persecuted around the world.

The ability to get angry about the right things at the right time in the right way is one sign of good mental health. Paul didn't lose his temper, but on the other hand he didn't turn away and say, "Well, it's a beautiful city. I think I'll go somewhere else and preach." He wasn't fooled by the splendor of Athens. He saw behind the beauty to the emptiness of idol worship. Then he determined to do something about it.

So Paul now takes on Athens. It's David versus Goliath all over again. Only this time there's one David surrounded by a thousand Goliaths.

Debating in the Synagogue

"So he reasoned in the synagogue with the Jews and the God-fearing Greeks, as well as in the marketplace day by day with those who happened to be there" (Acts 17:17). This verse reveals Paul's basic strategy in Athens. First, he started on the most familiar territory by going to the Jewish synagogue in Athens. There he reasoned with the Jews and the God-fearing Greeks. The word *reasoned* actually means "to debate." It has the idea of discussing issues of importance with a view to winning another person to your own point of view. This is not just a breezy chat where you give your opinion and I give mine and we both walk away happy. This was a serious debate over issues of eternal importance. In this case, it meant that Paul used the Old Testament to show the Jews and the God-fearing Greeks that Jesus was indeed the promised Messiah.

This was Paul's strategy everywhere he went. Since he himself was a Jew, it was only natural that he started by trying to reach his own people (cf. Rom. 9:1–3). He knew their language and shared the same background. He could "talk the talk" with the best of them. If they wanted to quote Rabbi So-and-so, Paul could answer that quote by quoting a half-dozen other rabbis. He knew the Old Testament as well as they did and he could debate it for hours, always with a view to leading his countrymen to faith in Christ.

Start Where You Are

Paul's first step makes sense for those who want to share Christ. Start where you are and reach the people who are nearest to you. Recently I had lunch with a man who directs Executive Ministries in the Chicago area for Campus Crusade for Christ. They set up meetings where top-level Christian businessmen and women can invite their unsaved friends to a banquet at a home or a nice hotel, have a lovely meal, and then hear a gifted speaker share Christ. Sometimes it's a sports figure or it might be a well-known business figure or a Christian from the political arena. In that kind of setting, high-powered businesspeople come to Christ because they feel comfortable hearing the gospel. As we ate lunch, I heard some amazing stories of highly-educated, highly-placed executives coming to Christ in great numbers through this ministry.

That was on Wednesday. On Thursday I spent two hours visiting Circle Urban Ministries. We walked through their buildings on Central Avenue in the Austin Community on the west side of Chicago. I saw with my own eyes the miracles being wrought in human lives through eleven separate ministries, including a medical clinic, a legal aid clinic, a tutoring program, a food pantry, and a Christian school. They are also reclaiming abandoned buildings used by drug dealers and gang members and turning them into affordable housing.

You could hardly find a cultural setting more different from the Executive Ministry of Campus Crusade. But the principle is exactly the same. You start where you are and you reach out to friends, your coworkers, your neighbors, and your family. Every summer Circle Urban Ministries reaches hundreds of people during their annual harvest festival when they put up a huge tent and have meetings, meals, and gospel services all day long for a week. That is good evangelism. It's peer to peer, friend to friend, family to family. Evangelism begins by reaching out to the people you know the best. That's what Paul did in Athens.

In the Marketplace

But Paul didn't stop there. Acts 17:17 says that he also discussed Christ in the marketplace with anyone he happened to meet. There's a particular name for the place where he went. In Greek it's called the Agora. If you go to Athens today, you'll find that the Agora is still there after two thousand years. It's a section of town near the Acropolis with narrow streets and lots of shops and restaurants crowded together. That's where people gathered in ancient Athens. Men and women would go to the Agora to shop, to meet their friends, to catch up on the latest news, and to discuss philosophy and religion.

That's where Paul went. But remember that he didn't know a single person in Athens. This wasn't like a Billy Graham crusade where they start three years in advance with a team of people moving into town to lay the groundwork for Mr. Graham. It's true that Paul had his team, but at this moment Timothy and Silas were somewhere else. Paul had to do his own advance work. Our text tells us that he went to the Agora day after day, chatting with anyone who would stop to talk to him. In doing this, he was following the practice of Socrates, who went to the same place several hundred years earlier to discuss philosophy using the Socratic method—questions and answers.

What do you do in a strange town when you want to share Christ? You find out where the action is and you go there. It's as simple as that. In our day, the place where the action is might be the mall, or it might be a college campus, or it might be an Internet discussion group, or it might be the cafeteria at lunch, or it might be around the water cooler, or it might be a public park, or it might be in the bleachers between innings at a Little League game.

Someday Soon

Each year our village sponsors an event called May Madness. The organizers close Main Street for several blocks and set up carnival rides and food stands. Various bands play from a number of makeshift stages. Always there are thousands of people milling around. One year a band called Someday Soon played on the central stage in the park at the center of all the festivities. Who or what is Someday Soon? It's a band made up of students who attend a youth group called Allied Force. For an hour they played Christian music—loudly! Since I know most of the teenagers, I went to give them support. It's not my style of music, which is good because the audience was almost entirely under the age of twenty. They chose music that talked about the need to know Jesus Christ personally. At the end of their set, one young man told the audience that the band was all about relationships—and that the most important relationship in the world is knowing God.

As I looked around the park, I saw lots of people who have no interest in visiting the church I pastor. And yet there they were, listening to Christian music in the center of our village.

I think the apostle Paul would heartily approve. He might not understand the music, but he would approve taking the gospel out into the marketplace of life. That day in Oak Park, May Madness was an agora—a place where ideas could be presented and discussed. Those teenagers were doing exactly what Paul did when he visited Athens two thousand years ago.

Cleverly Disguised Missionaries

What does all this mean for us today? I want to suggest one primary application: Every Christian is a missionary just like Paul, only most of us are cleverly disguised as something else. Paul was a missionary who didn't look like a missionary. He looked like a Jew from Tarsus, which is what he was. And for all anyone knew, he was just one more visitor coming to see the glories of Athens and to gaze on the splendor of its architecture and join in the philosophical discussions. When people saw Paul, they didn't think, "Aha! There's a missionary. I can spot one a mile away."

That's a key point, isn't it? The best missionaries don't look like missionaries at all. Paul looked like a tourist, and no one knew differently until he opened his mouth. Then suddenly everyone knew he was a man on a mission from God. The same should be true of you and me.

One evening while I was crossing the street near the center of Oak Park, a woman with three children stopped me and said, "Hi, Pastor Ray." I didn't recognize her until she said her name. She invited me to stop by and visit the cheesecake shop she and her husband operated several blocks away. We chatted for a bit and then she went one way and I went another. A few minutes later I was walking home when I passed by their shop. I went inside and immediately noticed a sign above the counter with two verses from Proverbs and a point to ponder. They put it where every customer was bound to see it. Her husband greeted me and told me about their business. Soon she came in and explained the sign on the chalkboard. Lots of people comment about it—most like it, but some people have said, "That offends me," and they leave the store. A close friend once asked, "Why do you have that sign? You're not in the ministry." "Oh yes we are," she replied. "This is our ministry."

Should I Talk to an Atheist?

She's right. She and her husband are missionaries cleverly disguised as the proprietors of a cheesecake store. They look just like everyone else until you go in their store, and then you discover they're undercover missionaries for Jesus who happen to sell cheesecake on the side.

It's the same with all of us. We're all missionaries. Some of us are cleverly disguised as doctors, teachers, sales reps, athletes, secretaries, nurses, lawyers, professors, homemakers, senior citizens, junior high school students, high school students, college students, graduate students, small business owners, administrators, shift workers, plant managers, and department heads. On and on the list goes. If someone asks you, "What do you do?" there's only one biblical answer: "I'm a missionary for Jesus Christ cleverly disguised as _____."

After a worship service, a woman told me that she had been talking with a friend who says he is an atheist. She also said that her Christian friends advised her not to talk to him again because he could drag her down spiritually. She wanted to know if she should talk to him even though he is an atheist. What do you think Paul would say? If we all refuse to talk to non-Christians, how will they ever hear the gospel? If they don't hear the gospel, how will they ever be saved?

In an earlier chapter I mentioned my friend Steve Meyer and his battle with a serious form of cancer. As I write these words he has finished the bone-marrow transplant and is now home recovering. When I went to see him in the hospital, he was only a few days past the transplant procedure. To be perfectly honest, he looked awful, and that's putting it mildly. His hair had fallen out, he was bloated from the radiation, and he appeared to have a very bad suntan from the radiation that destroyed his bone marrow. His voice was barely a whisper. For two or three days he had lived on morphine to handle the pain. But now he was feeling a bit better.

Steve wanted me to read an E-mail from his stepdaughter. She was engaged to be married, but her fiancé was not a born-again

Christian even though he had been raised in a Christian church. Two nights earlier she and her fiancé had come by to visit Steve in the hospital. She went with her mother to the cafeteria, leaving Steve and her fiancé alone. They struck up a conversation, and Steve asked him if he knew Christ as his personal Savior. He didn't. So Steve proceeded to explain the gospel to him—right there in the bone-marrow transplant unit at Rush Presbyterian Hospital in Chicago. When he finished, they prayed together and the young man trusted Christ as his Savior. Several weeks later this young man came to see me on Sunday morning, his face filled with the joy of one who has found new life in Christ.

What struck me as Steve told this story was his excitement at how God had opened the door for him to share Christ. He was fighting for his own life, but the only thing he wanted to talk about was how his future son-in-law had found the Lord.

Sharing Christ isn't about how much you know; it's about taking the natural opportunities God gives you to tell someone else the Good News. All you need to do is start where you are and walk through the doors as God opens them one by one. There are hungry hearts all around, ready to listen if only someone would care enough to share Christ with them.

The cities and towns of today look a lot like Athens in the New Testament. They have become havens for every strange "ism" of modern life. This generation is on the cutting edge of societal evolution—and it's not always a pretty picture. If Paul were to visit your town, he would be provoked for the same reason he was provoked in Athens. Lives are being ruined by idolatry, and people worship idols because they do not know the living God.

Do we care? Are our hearts stirred as Paul's was? What you look for determines what you see. Some people see art; Paul saw idols. Our challenge is the same today. The Lord Jesus can't be here in person so he's delegated you and me to represent him where we live. Open your eyes. Look around. You can't reach everyone, but you can reach someone. Start where you are and you will be surprised as God leads you to hungry hearts and open doors. On every hand people need the Lord. Who will tell them if we don't?

A Truth to Remember:
Every Christian is a missionary just like Paul, only most of us are cleverly disguised as something else.

Going Deeper

1. The world has come to us. Think about your friends, neighbors, acquaintances, coworkers, and classmates. How many different nationalities and ethnic groups are represented in your own circle of influence? As far as you know, how many of them have a religious background different from your own?

2. How would you answer a person who says, "The Bible may be the Word of God for you, but it's not the Word of God for me"?

3. Name some of the "idols" of contemporary society. Which ones stir up your spirit to anger and sorrow? Why?

4. Think about your city, your town, your neighborhood, your classroom, your dormitory. Name three of the prevailing spiritual values of the people who live in your contemporary "Athens." How much (or how little) do they understand about the gospel of Jesus Christ?

5. Name five creative ways you could "start where you are" in reaching others for Christ. Then write down the names of five people you would like to see come to Christ. Ask God to show you where you should begin in sharing your faith with them.

6. Complete this phrase: "I'm a missionary for Jesus Christ cleverly disguised as _____."

Taking Action

Before reading any further, take a shot at the imaginary scenario from the first part of this chapter. You've just gotten off the plane in some great city of the world. As far as you know, you are the first Christian ever to visit. And you are by yourself. What will you do? Where will you begin? What strategy will you follow?

Chapter 11

WHAT HAPPENS
WHEN WE DIE?

We live in a time when there is great fascination about life after death.

- A few years ago Raymond Moody wrote a best-seller called *Life after Life* that detailed the near-death experiences of men and women who "died" and then came back to tell stories of weightlessness, bright lights, and reunions with loved ones.

- Hundreds of so-called "channelers" claim to be able to contact the spirits of the dead.

- The New Age movement has popularized such Eastern concepts as the transmigration of souls, reincarnation (thanks especially to Shirley MacLaine), spiritualism, and communication with the dead.

- Video games featuring witches and sorcerers have captured the fascination of millions of school-age children.

- Today, via the Internet, anyone with a computer and modem can connect with online psychics, spirit guides, and experts in reincarnation. Using a search engine, I discovered that there are more than 40,000 Internet sites about witchcraft, 37,000 about sorcery, 20,000 about reincarnation, 10,000 about psychics, 14,000 about clairvoyance, and 6,000 about necromancy. Nearly all these sites are free and easy to access.

Why this fascination with the world beyond the grave? Is it not because death is so final? Whatever one thinks about the reports of "near-death" visions, death when it finally comes is irreversible. When you finally cross the line, there is no coming back from the other side. Death wins the battle every time. After the doctors have tried the latest wonder drug, after the best minds have pooled their wisdom, after the philosophers have done their best to explain that death is only a natural part of life, we come face to face with the ugly reality that someday we will all die. And that death—whether planned or accidental, whether comfortable or painful—will be the end of life as we have known it.

Three Great Questions

Nothing is certain—except death and taxes. But death is more certain than taxes. A clever person can find ways to evade taxes, but no one evades the Grim Reaper. When your time is up, it's up. Death can be postponed but never eliminated. Someday I will die, and those I love the most will die, and nothing can change this solemn fact. There is a parting at the end of the way. We all have a rendezvous with death.

No wonder the human mind is drawn to the question, "What happens when we die?" In many ways it is the one remaining unanswered question. We know so much about so many things, but about life after death we know very little.

There are three great questions every person must answer:

1. Where did I come from?
2. Why am I here?
3. Where am I going?

It is the third question that most grips the heart of man, for in one sense, the question "Where did I come from?" is yesterday's news, and the question "Why am I here?" is one that we answer every day, but the third question takes us into the unseen future—into the unfolding years and decades. What happens when we die? Is death the end of everything? Does man live for a few years and then simply vanish from the screen? Do we simply play our part and then shuffle off the stage into the misty obscurity of nothingness? Or is there something more, something beyond the great divide? Thousands of years ago Job spoke for the rest of us when he asked, "If a man dies, will he live again?" (Job 14:14).

Contrasting Destinies

In answering questions about life after death, we are left with only two sources to consult. Either we turn to human experience or we turn to the Word of God. If we turn to human experience, we find many guesses, many ideas, many theories—but no sure answers. That's because, in the nature of the case, no human has a sure answer. The only people who have the answer are dead! That leaves us with the Word of God. In God's Word we find ample, abundant answers. God who knows the future knows what happens when we die, and he hasn't left us to wonder about it. The Bible is filled with information on this subject, so much in fact that we can offer only a brief survey in this chapter.

If you want the answer in one sentence here it is: What happens after you die depends on what happens before you die. Consider what the Bible says in Hebrews 9:27, "It is appointed for men to die once, but after this the judgment" (NKJV). This is an appointment no one will miss. As someone has noted, the statistics on death are appalling. One hundred out of one hundred people will eventually die. We are all terminally ill with a disease called death; we just don't know when the end will come.

One Hundred Sixteen Others the Same Day

As I pondered this, my mind was drawn to the death of a former elder and beloved friend of many people in our congregation. He died just short of his forty-third birthday. On the day of his funeral I found his obituary in the *Chicago Tribune*. I counted one hundred sixteen other death notices that same day.

Death is no respecter of persons. Perhaps you've heard the story of Bill and George who were both avid baseball players. One day they wondered if people played baseball in heaven. They agreed that whoever died first would find out the answer and try to come back to communicate with the survivor. Eventually Bill died. Several weeks later George was awakened with a vision of his friend Bill. He was delighted to see him and asked, "Do they play baseball in heaven?" Bill said, "I've got good news and bad news. The good news is, they play baseball all the time in heaven. The bad news is, you're scheduled to pitch next week."

And we all laugh when we read about the friendly undertaker who signed all his correspondence, "Eventually yours." He's right, of course. Death is coming—eventually for all of us, sooner than we think for some of us.

Questions and Answers about Death

Before we go further, let's stop and think about some important questions that people often ask about death and dying.

Is There a "Second Chance" after Death?

This is the popular view of many people who hope that those who did not accept Christ in this life will somehow have a second chance after death—either in the afterlife or perhaps through reincarnation. The answer is quite simple: There is no biblical support whatsoever for the notion of a "second chance." Hebrews 9:27 declares that we die once and after that comes the judgment of God. Let no one be mistaken on this point. The only opportunity you will ever have to get right with God is the opportunity God affords you right now. If you dream of coming to God after you die, you are nursing a vain hope.

What about "Near-Death Experiences"?

Such experiences are very popular today. I've already mentioned the pioneering work of Raymond Moody. Other books in recent years have purported to tell of people who "died," went to "heaven," and then were given a "second chance" to return to the earth. Some of those books have been extremely popular, and a few have been embraced by Christians. However, a close inspection shows that most of those books embrace unbiblical heresy, either the notion that we are saved by doing good works or the idea that everyone is going to heaven in the end.

In thinking about this question, we need biblical balance. On one hand it's undeniably true that some Bible characters did see the Lord before they died. Stephen saw Jesus just before he died in Acts 7. Paul was evidently given a vision of heaven—perhaps during his stoning at Lystra in Acts 14. He alludes to the event in 2 Corinthians 12. However, it's important to say that such revelations did not happen often even in Bible times. Not every believer had or will have a revelation of heaven. Could such a thing happen today? Yes, but we shouldn't expect it or base our hope of heaven upon a last-second experience.

Let's also remember that Satan is the great deceiver. He can create scenes that seem to be scenes of heaven but are actually creations born in hell. Some near-death experiences are demonic in nature. You should never base your hope of heaven—or the hope of seeing a loved one in heaven—on a supposed vision or revelation. The only reliable ground given to us is the eternal, unchanging Word of God.

What Happens to Children Who Die?

This is obviously a very tender subject to many people. Parents want to know: Will I see my child again? The place to begin in answering this question is with the observation that the Bible doesn't specifically address this question. However, we do know two things are true. First, children are not born innocent, but sinful. If children who die do go to heaven—and I believe they do—it is not because they are morally innocent in the sight of God. All of us are born with an inclination to sin that leads us away from God. Ephesians 2:1 says that we are spiritually dead by nature. That applies as much to young children as it does to adults. Second, we know that God's grace is always greater than human sin. Romans 5:20 reminds us that where sin abounded, grace superabounded. God's grace always goes far beyond sin's disgrace.

I believe that God's grace credits children with the merits of Jesus' blood and righteousness so that children who die before they are old enough to believe are covered by his blood, and their entrance into heaven is made sure and certain. Thus they are saved by grace exactly as we are.

Can We Contact the Dead after They Are Gone?

The answer is no. Any attempt to dabble in spirit contact is strictly forbidden in the Bible. It is sometimes called necromancy or sorcery or dealing with familiar spirits. Remember, demons can masquerade as the dead. They can even mimic the voices of our loved ones and give information that only the dead person would have known (for more on this subject, see Lev. 19:26–28, 31; Deut. 18:9–14; Gal. 5:20). In case this isn't clear, let me make it plain. Do not attempt to contact the dead through any means at all—seances, parlor games, crystal balls, psychic readers, channelers, or mediums. You are involving yourself in that which God forbids. Leave the dead alone.

What Do You Say to Someone Who Has Lost a Loved One?

Over the years I have discovered that it really doesn't matter what you say in terms of the precise words. Those who are grieving will not remember the words you say, but they will never forget that you cared enough to be there when they needed you. If you go with God's love in your heart, he will give you any words you need to say. That means we don't need to answer questions only God can answer. If we don't know the spiritual state of the deceased, we shouldn't speculate, either to offer false hope or lay a heavier burden on those who are left behind. God is both just and merciful, and in every case he will do what is right.

What Happens at the Moment of Death . . .

Now we come to the central question: What happens at the very moment of death? I have already given the general answer: *What happens when you die depends on what happens before you die.* The Bible classifies the whole human race into two broad categories—the saved and the lost. The saved are those who have trusted Jesus Christ as Lord and Savior. The lost are those who haven't. What happens to the saved is radically different from what happens to the lost.

. . . For the Saved

The Bible is abundantly clear on this point. When the saved die, they go directly into the presence of the Lord. At this point we remember the words of Jesus to the thief on the cross, "I tell you the truth, *today* you will be with me in paradise" (Luke 23:43, emphasis added). This appears to be a straightforward promise that at the moment of death the repentant thief would pass from his life of crime and his agonizing death into the realm called "paradise." This would seem to contradict the teaching called "soul-sleep," which implies that at death a believer "sleeps" in a kind of suspended animation until the day of the resurrection. How could the thief be that very day in paradise if his soul went to sleep when he died? At the moment of death the believer passes immediately into the personal presence of Jesus Christ. This is our hope and comfort as we stand at the graveside of a loved one.

Paul said he had a desire "to depart and be *with Christ,* which is better by far" (Phil. 1:23, emphasis added). He also said, "We are confident, I say, and would prefer to be away from the body (that is, separated from the body by death) and *at home with the Lord*" (2 Cor. 5:8, emphasis added). These are the words of a man who believed that heaven would begin at the moment of his death. Was Paul looking forward to an unconscious slumber after his death? No! He was looking forward to the personal presence of Jesus Christ.

But that's not the whole story. The soul goes to be with the Lord in heaven, and the body is buried until the day of resurrection when Jesus returns to the earth. First Thessalonians 4:14 says, "We believe that Jesus died and rose again and so we believe that God will bring with Jesus those who have fallen asleep in him." Here you have both sides of the truth. Christians who die are said to be "with Jesus" (that's the soul in the conscious presence of the Lord) and "have fallen asleep in him" (that's the body which "sleeps" in the grave). Listen to Paul's description of that great reunion of body and soul: "For the Lord himself will come down from heaven, with a loud command, with the voice of the archangel and with the trumpet call of God, *and the dead in Christ will rise first*" (1 Thess. 4:16, emphasis added). Here is a clear promise of future bodily resurrection for the believer.

First Corinthians 15:51–55 adds the crucial fact that our bodies will be "raised imperishable"—that is, with a body that is perfect in every way, free from the vestiges of death and decay. In this life our bodies wear out, like a clock continually running down, but when we are raised, it will be with bodies that can never decay, never wear out, never suffer injury, never grow old, never get sick, and thank God, never die.

Many Christians have a wrong view of death. We think we're going from the land of living to the land of dying. But the opposite is true. If you know Jesus, you are going from the land of dying to the land of the living. Here are some of the images the Bible uses for the death of a Christian: going to sleep and waking up in heaven . . . moving from a tent to a mansion . . . walking from the darkness into a well-lit room . . . coming home to see your family and friends . . . being set free from prison . . . taking a long journey to a new land . . . riding a chariot to the New Jerusalem . . . moving into a brand-new home . . . opening a gate to a brand-new world.

Christians have always faced death with confidence. The very word *cemetery* comes from a Greek word meaning "sleeping-place," which refers to their confidence in the promise of the resurrection. Many pagans cremated their dead because they saw no further use for the human body. But Christians buried their dead as a statement of faith in the coming resurrection of the body. I have been asked more than once how God can raise the dead if the body has been burned or lost or vaporized in some terrible explosion. I don't think that's a difficult question at all. If you can raise the dead, you can raise the dead. Resurrection is God's problem, not ours. We don't need to know the *how* of the resurrection as long as we know the *who*.

As he lay dying, D. L. Moody proclaimed, "Earth recedes, heaven opens before me." Catherine Booth, wife of the founder of the Salvation Army, cried out, "The waters are rising, but I am not sinking." And George MacDonald, the English novelist, said, "I came from God, and I'm going back to God, and I won't have any gaps of death in the middle of my life." John Wesley summed up the faith of the early Methodists with four simple words: "Our people die well."

When Benjamin Franklin was twenty-three years old, he wrote the following epitaph. His words catch the essence of the Christian doctrine of bodily resurrection:

The body of
Benjamin Franklin
Printer;
Like the cover of an old book,
Its contents torn out,
And stripped of its lettering and gilding,
Lies here, food for worms.
But the work shall not be wholly lost:
For it will, as he believed, appear once more,
In a new and more elegant edition,
Revised and corrected
By the Author.

Once our bodies are raised, we will be with the Lord forever. Wherever he is, there we will be, rejoicing, praising, singing, and celebrating throughout the ages of eternity. First Thessalonians 4:17 says, "We will be with the Lord forever." Speaking of his own return, Jesus said, "In my Father's house are many rooms; if it were not so, I would have told you. I am going there to prepare a place for you. And if I go and prepare a place for you, I will come back and take you to be with me *that you also may be where I am*" (John 14:2–3, emphasis added).

What is ahead for us when we die?

- Our soul goes into the conscious presence of the Lord.
- Our body is buried until the day of resurrection.
- When Christ returns, we will be raised bodily from the grave.
- Body and soul reunited, we will be with the Lord forever.

As Tony Evans says, "Have a good time at my funeral, because I'm not going to be there."

. . . For the Lost

Now we turn to briefly consider the fate of those who die without Jesus Christ. The lost fear death and with good reason. Job 18:14

calls death "the king of terrors." Hebrews 2:14 reminds us that the devil holds people in bondage through the fear of death. And 1 Corinthians 15:26 calls death "the last enemy."

Before saying any more, we should note one similarity between the fate of the saved and the lost. At the moment of death, the body is buried in the grave while the soul enters a new realm. For the believer, the moment of death brings him into the personal presence of Christ. For the unbeliever, death begins an experience of unending conscious punishment.

We can summarize the fate of the lost in four short statements:

1. *At the moment of death the soul of the lost is sent to hell where it is in conscious torment.* In Luke 16:19–31 Jesus told of a rich man who upon his death went to hell and suffered in the flames of torment. It does not matter whether you think this passage is literal or figurative. If you say it is literal, then it must be a terrible punishment. If it is figurative, the figure itself is so awful to consider that the reality must be much worse.

2. *That punishment is eternal.* Though this is debated in some circles today, Christians have united across the centuries in their belief that the Bible teaches an eternal punishment for those who do not know our Lord. Mark 9:43–48 speaks of the fire that is not quenched and the worm that does not die—a reference to the continuing existence of human personality in hell.

3. *The body is raised at the Great White Throne judgment.* Revelation 20:11–15 describes the awesome scene as the unsaved dead are raised to stand before God and receive their final sentence of doom.

4. *The unsaved are then cast into the lake of fire where they will reside forever, eternally separated from the presence of Almighty God.* If this is unbearable to think about, if we shrink from such a thought, then let us by all means do whatever is necessary to make sure that such a fate does not befall us or the ones we love the most.

This is the final destiny of those who do not know Jesus Christ. To make it more personal, it is the final destiny of your friends and neighbors, your loved ones, your parents, your brothers, your sisters, your children, if they die without Jesus Christ. And it is your destiny if you die without Jesus Christ. Let that thought linger in your mind. The reality of hell is more than just a theoretical doctrine. There is a place reserved for you in the lake of fire unless you by a conscious choice put your complete trust in Jesus Christ as your Lord and Savior.

Dr. Barnhouse and the Shadow of Death

Only one question remains. How can you personally face your own death with confidence? Dr. Donald Grey Barnhouse—beloved Bible teacher of another generation—told the following story. While he was still a young man in the ministry, his first wife died. As he was returning from the funeral with his heartbroken children, their car came to a stoplight just as a massive truck pulled up next to them, blocking the light of the sun. Seeing the immense shadow that had overtaken them, Dr. Barnhouse asked his children if they would rather be run over by the truck or by the shadow of the truck. "By the shadow," the children instantly replied, knowing that a shadow could not hurt them. "That's what has happened to your mother," he told them. "Death cannot hurt her because the Lord Jesus Christ took her to heaven. It is only the shadow of death that took her from us."

If you know Jesus, you have nothing to fear when death knocks at your door. Death comes to all of us—it will come for you one of these days. Do you know Jesus? If so, then you need not live in fear. Death may be quick or slow, painful or painless, but when the moment comes, you will find yourself ushered into heaven where you will see Jesus face to face.

Some people wonder if they will have enough faith when they die. They worry about losing their faith and wonder if that will cause

God to turn them away. When she was a young child in Holland Corrie ten Boom worried about her own death and whether or not she would have enough courage when the moment finally came. Her father—Papa ten Boom—knew of her fears and calmed her heart with these words: "Corrie, when I am going to take you on the train, when do I give you the ticket?" "Just before we get on board." "That's right. Dying is like taking a trip to see the Lord Jesus. He will give you whatever you need just when you need it. If you don't have the courage now, it's because you don't need it now. When you need it, the Lord will give it to you, and you won't be afraid."

In another generation, believers talked about "dying grace." They meant the special enablement God gives to his children as death draws near. Countless Christians who worried about their last moments on earth have exited this life full of faith because the Lord gave them grace just when they needed it most.

Jesus Has the Keys

Here are the words of Jesus in Revelation 1:18: "I am the Living One; I was dead, and behold I am alive for ever and ever! And I hold the keys of death and Hades." Keys are a sign of authority. If you have the keys to my house, you can open it and go in anytime you want. It is often said that the devil owns the gates of hell—that is, he has the power of death. But that's okay. The devil has the gates, but Jesus has the keys. We have nothing to fear in the moment of death for when the time comes, Jesus will personally unlock the gate and usher us into his presence.

"I am the resurrection and the life. He who believes in me will live, even though he dies; and whoever lives and believes in me will never die. Do you believe this?" (John 11:25). If you believe in Jesus, you will never die. What an amazing promise. But believers die every day. Yes, but for the believer, death is merely the passing from this life with all its sorrows into life eternal in the presence of our Lord. The question is not: What happens when we die? But rather: What will happen when you die?

Death is not the *end* of the road, it is only a *bend* in the road. For the believer, death is the doorway to heaven. For the unbeliever, it is a passageway into unimaginable suffering. These things are true even if we do not fully understand them. They are true even if we don't believe them.

What happens when you die depends on what happens before you die. Here is my final word to you: Make sure you're ready to die so that when the time comes, you won't be surprised by what happens next.

A Truth to Remember:
What happens when you die depends on what happens before you die.

Going Deeper

1. Have you ever had a near-death experience, or do you know anyone who has? Why is it crucial that such experiences always be evaluated by the standard of God's Word?

2. Why does the Bible contain such strong warnings against trying to contact the spirits of the dead? What happens when those warnings are ignored?

3. Picture the moment of your own death. How do you expect it will happen? Do you fear that moment? Describe what will happen to you the first five minutes after your death.

4. Do you believe in the resurrection of the dead? Why is this doctrine essential to the Christian faith? Name at least five Christians now dead who will be raised when Christ returns.

5. Read 1 Corinthians 15:35–58 and Revelation 20:11–15. What does the first passage teach about the resurrection of the saved? What does the second passage teach about the resurrection of the lost?

6. Do you believe in a place called hell where unbelievers are punished for eternity? Why or why not? Why is this doctrine sometimes denied today?

Taking Action

Take a moment to calculate the number of days you have lived so far. Now take a guess as to how many more days you expect to live. What is the most eternally profitable way you can spend your remaining days?

Chapter 12

WHAT IS HEAVEN LIKE?

Here are two statements that seem to be almost universally true: Everyone wants to know about heaven, and everyone wants to go there. Recent polls suggest that nearly 80 percent of all Americans believe there is a place called heaven.[15] I find that statistic encouraging because it tells me that even in this skeptical age there is something deep inside the human heart that cries out, "There's got to be something more." Something more than the pain and suffering of this life. Something more than seventy or eighty years on planet earth. Something more than being born, living, dying, and then being buried in the ground. I believe there is also a "heaven-shaped vacuum" inside every heart, a sense that we were made for something more than this life. We were made to live forever somewhere. In a real sense, we were made for heaven.

There is another fascinating statistic I should mention. Not only do most Americans believe in heaven; most people expect to go there when they die. If you took a microphone to the streets of any major city and asked, "Do you think you will go to heaven when you die?" the vast majority of people would answer, "I hope so," or "I think so," or perhaps "I think I've got a good chance." Not very many people would say they aren't going to heaven.

Perhaps one modest point is in order. Whenever you talk about living forever somewhere, it would help to know for sure where you are going. After all, if you're wrong about heaven, you're going to be wrong for a long, long time.

With that as background, I turn now to consider some of the most frequently asked questions about heaven. But before I jump in, I should make one preliminary point. The only things we can know for certain about heaven are the things revealed in the Bible. Everything else is just speculation and hearsay. The Bible tells us everything we need to know, and I believe it also tells us everything we can know for certain about heaven.[16]

Where Is Heaven?

There are three things I can tell you in answer to this question. The most important fact is that heaven is a real place. Listen to the words of Jesus on the night before he was crucified: "Do not let your hearts be troubled. Trust in God; trust also in me. In my Father's house are many rooms; if it were not so, I would have told you. I am going there to prepare *a place* for you. And if I go and prepare *a place* for you, I will come back and take you to be with me that you also may be where I am" (John 14:1–3, emphasis added).

Twice in three verses Jesus calls heaven a place. He means that heaven ("my Father's house") is a real place, as real as New York, London, or Chicago. The place called heaven is just as real as the place you call home. It's a real place filled with real people, which is why the Bible sometimes compares heaven to a mansion with many rooms (John 14:1–3) and sometimes to an enormous city teeming with people (Rev. 21–22).

The Bible also tells us that heaven is the dwelling place of God. His throne is there, the angels are there, and the Lord Jesus Christ is in heaven. Philippians 3:20 says very plainly that "our citizenship is in heaven. And we eagerly await a Savior from there, the Lord Jesus

Christ." That's why Jesus told the thief on the cross, "Today you will be with me in paradise" (Luke 23:43).

Third, the Bible hints that heaven is not as far away as we might think. Because heaven is a real place, we sometimes think it must be outside our present universe—which would mean that it is billions and billions of light years away. However, it's very clear that the early Christians understood that they would pass immediately from this life into the presence of Christ in heaven. How can that be possible if heaven is beyond the farthest galaxy?

Hebrews 12:22–24 tells us something amazing about what the gospel has done for us: "But you have come to Mount Zion, to the heavenly Jerusalem, the city of the living God. You have come to thousands upon thousands of angels in joyful assembly, to the church of the firstborn, whose names are written in heaven. You have come to God, the judge of all men, to the spirits of righteous men made perfect, to Jesus the mediator of a new covenant, and to the sprinkled blood that speaks a better word than the blood of Abel."

The writer is here comparing Mt. Sinai with Mt. Zion. Under the old covenant no one could come near God except under very strict conditions. That's why the mountain shook with thunder and lightning. But now in Christ we have been brought near to heavenly realities.[17] Think of what he is saying:

- We're not that far from heaven.
- We're not that far from the angels.
- We're not that far from our loved ones in heaven.
- We're not that far from God.
- We're not that far from Jesus himself.

Hebrews 12 tells us that we have been brought very near to ultimate spiritual reality through Jesus Christ. We are in his presence, surrounded by angels, enrolled in heaven, accepted by God, not far from our loved ones, forgiven by the blood. We have something wonderful in Jesus. We live next door to heaven. All the unseen world is open to us. Not sometimes, but all the time. In Christ we have come near to God and Jesus and the church and the angels and our loved ones and Mount Zion and heaven itself.

Heaven is a real place, it's where Jesus is right now, and it's not far away from us. For most of us this earth seems so real that we can hardly imagine any other world. But as the years pass and our loved ones leave this life, we begin to realize that true reality must be somewhere else. As the saints of God go to heaven, we find ourselves thinking more about heaven and less about the earth until, if we live long enough, we have more friends in heaven than we do on earth. The best view of heaven comes when we have loved ones in the city of light.

What Is Heaven Like?

This question came from a junior high student. I would answer by saying that the Bible doesn't give us a great deal of information. What we have are images and pictures of heaven and comparisons with life on earth.

What is heaven like? Here are some biblical facts about heaven. It is . . .

- God's dwelling place (Ps. 33:13),
- where Christ is today (Acts 1:11),
- where Christians go when they die (Phil. 1:21–23),
- the Father's house (John 14:2),
- a city designed and built by God (Heb. 11:10),
- a better country (Heb. 11:16), and
- paradise (Luke 23:43).

Most of us have heard that heaven is a place where the streets are paved with gold, the gates are made of pearl, and the walls are made of precious jewels. Those images come from Revelation 21–22, which offers us the most extended picture of heaven in the entire Bible. If you ask me if I believe those things are literally true, the answer is yes and no. Yes, they are literally true but no, heaven won't be anything like we imagine. It will be much greater.

A delightful old legend tells of a rich man who showed up at the gate of heaven lugging a heavy suitcase with him. At first the attendant at the gate told him he couldn't come in. However, he begged and pleaded, saying he had brought some of his earthly wealth with him. The attendant thought for a moment and agreed to admit it on the condition that he search the suitcase first. When he opened it, he found that the rich man had stuffed it with bars of gold bullion. With an astonished look the attendant asked, "You brought pavement?" When John writes about a street paved with gold, I do not doubt his words. He simply reports what he saw in his vision. Thus his words are literally true. They are also meant to tell us that the things we value so highly in this life will be used to pave the roads in heaven.

Heaven is a real place filled with real people. The Bible pictures it as a great city filled with all of God's people.

What would such a city look like? It would be a city with . . .

- no pollution because the skies would always be crystal clear,
- no crime or violence because no criminals would ever enter,
- no greedy politicians, no drug pushers, no child molesters, and
- no potholes and no power outages either.

Heaven would be filled with abundant parks, rivers, rolling meadows, and flowing streams. Lining the streets would be flowers in constant bloom, fruit trees of every kind, and every species of plant life growing free from pestilence and disease.

The gates would be made of pearl, the walls of jasper, the streets of gold. Precious stones would lie on the ground like playthings—emeralds, rubies, diamonds galore. On every hand there would be children laughing, bright conversation, music floating from every direction.

In the city that God builds, there are no tears; there is no sorrow, no regret, no remorse. Bitterness gone forever, failure left far behind, suffering redeemed and rewarded. There are no eyeglasses, no braces, no wheelchairs, no false teeth, no bald heads, no hearing aids, and no crutches. There are no more hospitals, no more nursing homes, no paramedics, no CPR. Doctors have to find a new job; they aren't needed anymore. Aspirin gone, accidents over, cancer disappeared, heart attacks banished, AIDS a distant memory. In heaven no one grows old and feeble.

There is one other thing you won't find in heaven. There are no cemeteries in the city that God builds. Why? There are no funerals . . . because in that glad city no one ever dies. If you make it to that city, you live forever, never to die again. Either you believe in heaven or you don't. It's either a real place or it isn't. This is heaven—where all our best dreams finally come true.

Who Is in Heaven Right Now?

This question is not difficult to answer. God is in heaven because heaven is his dwelling place. The Lord Jesus has been in heaven ever since he ascended from the earth shortly after his resurrection (Acts 1:9–11). The Bible tells us that the angels are in heaven. In fact, there are myriads of angels—uncountable numbers of heavenly beings—all of them serving the Lord in various ways. And the saints of God who died on this earth are in heaven.[18] The Bible teaches that the moment we die we go directly into the presence of the Lord Jesus Christ. Paul spoke of this in 2 Corinthians 5:7–8 and Philippians 1:21–23.

But I do not want to be ambiguous on this point. Not everyone is in heaven now. Some people won't make it. The Bible speaks of the saved and the lost. The saved are those who trust Jesus Christ as their eternal Savior. The lost are those who do not trust Christ as Savior.

This is the great dividing line of humanity—you are either saved or you are lost. And there is no middle category. You will either spend eternity in heaven or eternity in hell.

One evening a man I do not know called to talk about the moral crisis engulfing our community. "You're on record," he said, "as saying you don't believe that people who disagree with you will go to hell." "That's right," I replied. "My job is not to decide who goes to heaven and who goes to hell. That's God's job. I'm in sales, not administration." It is enough to know what God has said about heaven and who will go there. The saved of all the ages will be there—and that vast throng will no doubt include many people who would surprise us if we knew it now. Certainly heaven will be more wonderful than our imagination and it's population more diverse than we expect.

But I am sure of this one truth: No one will go to heaven except by the grace of God and through the merits of the blood of Jesus Christ. Those who reject Christ have no hope of heaven.

Will We Know One Another in Heaven?

This is one of the most frequently asked questions about heaven. I would like to share an answer given by a Bible teacher of another generation—a man named William Pettingill.[19] He said, "We may be sure that we shall not know less in heaven than we know here." In proof he quotes 1 Corinthians 13:12: "Now we see but a poor reflection as in a mirror; then we shall see face to face. Now I know in part; then I shall know fully, even as I am fully known."

How does God know us? He knows us completely, intimately, thoroughly, inside and out, with nothing hidden but everything seen as it really is (Ps. 139:1–4; Heb. 4:12). When we get to heaven we'll know each other as God knows us because all the imperfections of this life will be removed. In this life sin causes us to cover ourselves—not just physically but emotionally and spiritually. But when sin is finally lifted from us, then we can be ourselves with no shame, no pain, no embarrassment, and no covering up. Pettingill concludes that we will know every person in heaven, and all of them will be friends and loved ones to us.

The Bible makes it clear that individual personality survives the grave. That's why Mary could recognize Jesus after his resurrection (John 20:16–18). Physical death ends our physical life, but it does not and cannot destroy the soul. That remains forever. In heaven I will be the same person then that I am now—only with all the imperfections and limitations of sin finally removed. This is a wonderful thought—that the essence of who we are will remain throughout eternity—yet vastly improved by God's grace.

That helps me think about a related question that people sometimes ask: How old will we be in heaven? I once heard a preacher say that we will all be thirty-three years old because that's approximately how old Jesus was when he died. Of course there is no scriptural support for that statement. The truth is, there won't be any age in heaven in the sense that we speak of age on the earth. Growing old is a function of the decaying effects of sin. I do not believe that babies who die in infancy will be babies for eternity nor do I believe that people who waste away from cancer will appear emaciated in heaven. It will be something else entirely—which I can barely explain and certainly do not understand.

In heaven we will know one another intimately. That's why Peter, James, and John recognized Moses and Elijah on the Mount of Transfiguration, even though Moses died and Elijah was taken directly to heaven hundreds of years earlier (Matt. 17:1–9). I don't think they had nametags on. There was something about those two men that made Peter, James, and John recognize them even though they had never seen them before. That's why a wife whose husband died when she was young will be able to pick her husband out of a crowd of billions of people, even though she hasn't seen him for fifty years since he died on the earth. In heaven she will say, "Sweetheart! I knew it was you." And he will know her.

How this can be I do not know, but I believe it to be true. In heaven there will be no strangers.

What Will We Do in Heaven?

A very honest junior high student put the question this way: "Worshiping God forever in heaven sounds boring—is it wrong to feel this? Is heaven going to be fun?" I think this student envisions heaven as one long church service that never ends. If so, I can understand the concern. Once again the Bible doesn't tell us everything we would like to know, but of this we can be sure: Heaven won't be boring, and it will be more fun than the best party you ever attended.

So what will we do for all eternity? The answer is, we're going to help God run the universe. Jesus told a parable about a man of noble birth who gave his servants money to invest. One servant had doubled his money, so the man said, "You will rule over ten cities." The next servant had seen a 50 percent increase, so his master said, "Rule over five cities." And the man who hid his money had even that amount taken from him in punishment (Luke 19:11–27).

The story is a picture of what heaven will be like. We will use our gifts to administer the new heaven and the new earth. Bakers will bake, teachers will teach, singers will sing, and I suppose that preachers will preach. For all I know, soldiers may march off to battle and quarterbacks will throw passes. Think of the flowers the botanists will study. Gifted astronomers will go from galaxy to galaxy studying the wonders of God's creation. We will use all our natural (and supernatural) gifts and talents in the service of God. Nothing will be wasted. I can guarantee that you won't be sitting around on a cloud eating grapes and polishing your halo. We'll all be too busy for that.

The best part of heaven will be seeing Jesus face to face. We will worship the Son of God and celebrate his great victory over sin while the endless ages of eternity roll on and on. The best music you've ever heard will pale compared to the music of heaven. The most awesome worship you've experienced on earth is but a dim reflection of the praise we will render around the throne of God.

How Can I Be Sure I Am Going to Heaven?

This is the most important question of all. Here is a wonderful truth: God has made it easy for you to go to heaven. He did the hard part when he sent his Son to die on the cross for you. He paid the price for your sins so that you could one day stand before God in heaven. Jesus said, "I am the way and the truth and the life. No one comes to the Father except through me" (John 14:6). He also said, "I am the door; if anyone enters through Me, he shall be saved" (John 10:9 NASB). Jesus is not only the way to heaven; he is also the door to heaven. If you want to go to heaven, you've got to go through the door marked "Jesus Christ." There is no other entrance.

Early in Ronald Reagan's first term as president, a number of evangelical leaders were invited to the White House to meet with him. During the meeting a well-known pastor asked the president, "Suppose you were to die and found yourself standing at the door of heaven. If God were to say, 'Why should I let you into heaven?' what answer would you give?"

Before I tell you how the president answered that question, let me ask how you would respond. Picture the scene. You are standing at the very gates of heaven. It's more beautiful than you ever dreamed possible. This is where you want to spend eternity. This is where you belong. But before you enter, the Lord himself asks what possible reason you have to claim admission. You pause, knowing that all eternity hangs on your answer. What will you say?

President Reagan paused, thought for a moment, then replied, "Well, I guess I'd have to answer with John 3:16, 'For God so loved the world, that he gave his only begotten Son, that whosoever believeth in him should not perish, but have everlasting life' " (KJV).

That is indeed a good answer because our only hope of heaven is through the Lord Jesus Christ.

What we need is solid ground on which to stand. And we have it in the death and resurrection of Jesus Christ. Our entire hope of heaven is wrapped up in what Jesus did when he died on the cross for the sins of the world and rose from the dead on Easter Sunday morning.

A beloved hymn by Edward Mote entitled "The Solid Rock" puts it this way:

My hope is built on nothing less
Than Jesus' blood and righteousness;
I dare not trust the sweetest frame,
But wholly lean on Jesus' name.
On Christ, the solid Rock, I stand;
All other ground is sinking sand,
All other ground is sinking sand.

That says it all. If you want to go to heaven, you must base your hope on the solid rock of Jesus' blood and righteousness. No one goes to heaven by accident. Heaven is God's prepared place for prepared people. We prepare for heaven and then God prepares heaven for us. I've already told you that most people believe in heaven and most people think they are going there. But are they on the right road? Are they building their lives on Jesus Christ—the solid rock? Too many, I fear, are standing on sinking sand and do not know it.

What is your hope for heaven? Mine is Jesus Christ. I've staked everything I have on him. If he can't take me to heaven, then I'm not going there. What about you? When the dark night falls, the lights go out, and the waters of death swirl around you, what will happen to you then? If you know Jesus, you have nothing to fear. Put your trust in Jesus. Run to the cross. Stand with your full weight on the solid rock of our salvation. May God help you to trust in Jesus Christ and him alone for your salvation. And may God grant that we will all meet one day in heaven.

Safe at home. In heaven at last. I'll be there. What about you?

A Truth to Remember:

**Heaven is a real place and it's not far
away from us.**

Going Deeper

1. "The only things we can know for certain about heaven are the things revealed in the Bible." Do you agree with this statement? Why or why not?

2. Are you surprised that most people expect to go to heaven? What does that say about the spiritual condition of this generation?

3. Do you expect to go to heaven? On what basis will God decide who goes to heaven and who goes to hell? According to Revelation 22:14–15, who enters heaven and who is left out?

4. How would you answer someone who says, "I believe everyone is going to heaven"?

5. If you could ask God one question about heaven, what would it be?

6. Do you tend to be more earthly-minded or more heavenly-minded? Name three ways your life would be different if you thought more about heaven than you do.

Taking Action

Using a concordance, look up every verse in the New Testament that mentions heaven. Make a list of the main facts you discover. From that list put together the "top ten things everyone needs to know about heaven." Share your "top ten" list with at least one other person. Better still, use it as the basis for a Sunday school class, a devotional, or a small-group Bible study.

Chapter 13

WHEN IS
JESUS COMING BACK?

A re we living in the last days before the return of Christ to the
earth? According to several recent polls, many people answer
yes. One survey reports that 66 percent of Americans believe that
Jesus Christ will return to earth someday—yet one third of those
people say they never attend church. A *Newsweek* magazine poll
reports that 45 percent of those surveyed believe that Jesus Christ will
return in their lifetime. The same poll reveals that 40 percent of those
surveyed believe the world will end in a battle at Armageddon
between Christ and Antichrist.[20]

It is easy to understand the current interest since we are the generation privileged to see the beginning of a new millennium. It would
be unique enough to see a new century—something reserved for our
grandparents or (more likely) our great-grandparents—but to witness
the passing of one millennium to another—that is something that no
one we know has ever seen and no one we know will ever see again.

Because we live at one of the rare breakpoints of history, many
people have speculated on what this moment means for humanity.
Some see the new millennium as the dawn of an era of peace and

international harmony. Others worry that the rapid growth of technology will lead to machines that can replicate themselves, ushering in an age in which a few people bent on doing evil can hold the world hostage. And many people, including some who rarely read the Bible, wonder if the "signs of the times" point to the imminent return of Jesus Christ.

None of this should surprise us since Christians have always believed in the Second Coming of Christ. Jesus himself declared, "I will come back" (John 14:3). And when Christ ascended into heaven, the angels promised the disciples that "this same Jesus, who has been taken from you into heaven, will come back in the same way you have seen him go into heaven" (Acts 1:11). Belief in the Second Coming has always been considered one of the fundamental truths of our faith. Even though we have often argued about the details surrounding his return, Christians of every denomination have agreed on this fact: Jesus Christ is coming again. By that we mean that Jesus himself ("this same Jesus") is coming back to the earth—physically, visibly, bodily, personally. The actual, historical figure who lived two thousand years ago on the other side of the world is returning to the earth one more time.

Coming Soon!

Here's an interesting corollary to that truth. Because Christians have always believed in the Second Coming, there have always been Christians who believed that Jesus would come back in their own lifetime. It's clear that the earliest Christians expected Christ to return to the earth while they were still alive. That's why the apostle Paul could say in 1 Thessalonians 4:16–17 that "the dead in Christ will rise first. After that, *we who are still alive and are left* will be caught up together with them in the clouds to meet the Lord in the air" (emphasis added). Paul never expected to have his head chopped off in Rome; he fervently thought that he would live to see the Second Coming.

Some Christians in every generation since then have believed the same thing. For instance, Christopher Columbus thought that his voyages were part of God's ordained plan and that Jesus would return in the year 1650 (or thereabouts). In the 1840s a man named William Miller convinced his followers to sell all their worldly goods because he believed that the Second Coming was at hand. The twentieth century has seen many similar predictions: 1914 (connected with World War I—"the war to end all wars") . . . 1975 (a date suggested by the Jehovah's Witnesses) . . . 1982 (connected with an unusual planetary conjunction) . . . 1988 (predicted by a Bible teacher who wrote a book that sold hundreds of thousands of copies) . . . 1994 (suggested by a prominent radio Bible teacher).

All these dates have this in common: They were all wrong. In fact, every date for the Second Coming that has been suggested over the last two thousand years has been proven wrong. That should tell us something.

During my first year in seminary, my wife and I served as youth directors at an outreach center in Dallas. Our duties consisted mainly of taking care of the children on Friday nights while their parents attended the Bible class at the same time. One night we were mobbed with children, so many that I wondered what was going on. When I went upstairs, I saw that the speaker that evening was addressing a crowd two or three times larger than usual. It turned out that someone had calculated that in 1982 there would be an unusual conjunction of the planets. It happened that this particular Friday night was exactly seven years to the day before the unusual planetary alignment would take place. Could it be possible that the rapture would take place that very night? The speaker would not go that far, but he clearly thought it was possible and emphasized that we should be prepared to meet Jesus whenever he comes. That night sticks in my mind as perhaps the very first time I ever truly believed that Jesus might come back soon.

Two Dangers

The same thing happened in late 1990 and early 1991 during the Gulf War crisis. As I talked with a friend about the massive military buildup in the Middle East, he remarked that "for the first time in my life I get up each day and think, 'Jesus might come back today.'"

We face two dangers whenever we talk about the Second Coming: (1) becoming more concerned about the date and the signs than about his return and (2) ignoring the truth of the Second Coming and living as though he will never return. Frankly, I don't know which is worse.

In Matthew 24–25 the Lord Jesus Christ gives us his longest statement about the events surrounding his return to the earth. Called the Olivet Discourse (because he spoke these words while standing on the Mount of Olives), the message begins with two questions from the disciples (24:1–3). Jesus first explains the signs of the whole age between his first and second comings (vv. 4–14). He then reveals specific events that will take place just prior to his return (vv. 15–28). Then he speaks of his return to the earth in great power and glory (vv. 29–31). In verse 32 Jesus begins to answer the question: When will these things happen? That answer continues to verse 41. Then in verses 42–51 Jesus reveals how his followers can be fully prepared for his return.

Four Facts from Jesus

When is Jesus coming back? Here are four facts to consider from the lips of the Lord Jesus Christ himself.

Fact #1: We Can Know the General Time but Not the Precise Moment

"Now learn this lesson from the fig tree: As soon as its twigs get tender and its leaves come out, you know that summer is near. Even so, when you see all these things, you know that it is near, right at the door. I tell you the truth, this generation will certainly not pass away until all these things have happened. Heaven and earth will pass away, but my words will never pass away. No one knows about that day or hour, not even the angels in heaven, nor the Son, but only the Father" (Matt. 24:32–36).

The story of the fig tree works on two levels. First, it is a truth from nature. When the leaves first begin to come out in the spring, we know that the summer is near. By the same token, when the signs of Matthew 24 begin to take place, then we will know the return of Christ cannot be far away. Second, the fig tree is a common biblical symbol for the nation of Israel (Hos. 9:10; Matt. 21:18–22). It may be that Jesus is alluding to the restoration of the nation of Israel in the end times. Historically, Israel ceased to exist as a nation after the destruction of Jerusalem by the Romans in A.D. 70. But in 1948 Israel became a nation once again. I believe that this restoration (though it is in unbelief) is the first step in the fulfillment of the prophecies of Ezekiel 36–39; Daniel 9:24–27; and Romans 11:26.

When Jesus says that "this generation" will not pass away until all the signs are fulfilled, I think he means that when the signs of the end do begin to occur, they will all come to a conclusion within the span of a generation. It helps to think of the signs of the Second Coming like streams flowing in a great river. If you go to northern Minnesota, you will see various streams and springs that are the headwaters of the Mississippi River. "But these are so small," you say. Indeed they are, but as other streams and tributaries feed into them, they will become the mighty Mississippi River that flows into the Gulf of Mexico.

In the same way one "sign" may not mean very much. But as more and more of them come together, they form a river leading us to the climax of human history. Those signs—which in some ways have always been present—will become more evident in the last days. In short, the generation that sees the predicted events of Matthew 24 begin to unfold will also see his return.

However, no one will ever know the precise moment of his return. No one can know the day or the hour. The best we can do is to read the signs and know that the time is at hand. If anyone ever tells you that they have pinpointed the year or the month or the day or the hour of Jesus' return, do not believe this claim. That person is either a false prophet or a seriously deluded Bible student. Jesus strictly forbids setting dates for his return.[21]

But of this much we may be sure: Jesus Christ is coming to earth again. You can take that to the bank. His return is more certain than the existence of the universe. Heaven and earth may pass away, but his Word—which in this context means the announcement of his return—will never pass away.

We can trust Jesus Christ to keep his Word! He is coming back.

Fact #2: Jesus Will Return at a Time When the World Is Completely Unprepared

"As it was in the days of Noah, so it will be at the coming of the Son of Man. For in the days before the flood, people were eating and drinking, marrying and giving in marriage, up to the day Noah entered the ark; and they knew nothing about what would happen until the flood came and took them all away. That is how it will be at the coming of the Son of Man. Two men will be in the field; one will be taken and the other left. Two women will be grinding with a hand mill; one will be taken and the other left" (Matt. 24:37–41).

Here Jesus makes a very simple comparison. As it was in the days of Noah, so it will be when Christ returns. What was it like in Noah's day? It was "business as usual." While Noah patiently built the ark and warned people of coming judgment, they laughed at him and said, "It will never happen." Noah's day was like our day—an age of skeptical unbelief and casual unconcern. The more Noah preached, the more his contemporaries mocked him. They refused to believe that anything like a worldwide flood was possible. The notion was so ridiculous that they could not take Noah seriously.

So for years and years life continued without a change—eating, drinking, marrying, giving in marriage. With each passing day Noah looked like more of a fool than the day before. But finally the heavens opened and the rains came down. When Noah entered the ark, I'm sure his friends pounded on the door and said, "Noah, we're sorry. You were right and we were wrong. Open up. Let us in." But it was too late.

"The flood came and took them all away." Think of it: an entire generation wiped out by the hand of God. One moment you're sitting down to eat supper, the next your home has been washed away. Perhaps you're at work in the field, then suddenly the field disappears under a wall of water. Where once there was a world, suddenly the world you knew has perished beneath the waves.

And it happened so suddenly that no one except Noah and his family was ready. Everyone else perished as the floodwaters rolled across the surface of the earth.

This is what the Second Coming will be like for an unbelieving world. It will be business as usual until the very day Jesus returns. Just as those who lived before the great flood did not believe Noah, even so the world mocks the idea that Jesus will return. They call it a myth, a legend, a nice fairy tale, but they don't believe it will really happen.

And just as the flood brought sudden judgment to the world, the return of Christ will do the same. When the waters came, the unbelievers were "taken" in sudden death so that only Noah and his family were left. When Jesus returns to the earth, unbelievers will once again be "taken" in death and judgment, and only believers will be preserved by God. And just as the ark saved Noah, even so Jesus Christ is the "ark of safety" for those who believe in him.

These verses teach us that this present age will end in sudden, dramatic judgment and a complete and final separation of the saved and the lost. The world will not expect it and will, therefore, be completely unprepared.

Fact #3: We Are Called to Be Ready Because Jesus May Return at Any Moment

"Therefore keep watch, because you do not know on what day your Lord will come. But understand this: If the owner of the house had known at what time of night the thief was coming, he would have kept watch and would not have let his house be broken into. So you also must be ready, because the Son of Man will come at an hour when you do not expect him" (Matt. 24:42–44).

Note the two main commands: "Keep watch" and "Be ready." This summarizes how believers should view the Second Coming of Christ. Theologians often speak of the imminent return of Christ. The word *imminent* means "at any moment." He could have come yesterday, he might come today, he may come tomorrow, he definitely will come someday.

How does a thief come to your house? Sudden and unannounced. After all, if you knew a thief was coming at 3:15 A.M. on Thursday morning, you would be ready for him, but thieves rarely call and make appointments in advance. "I'll try to be there by 3:15, but it might be closer to 4:00 because we've got two other houses to rob, but it would help if you would just pile the stuff in the middle of the floor so we don't have to search through all your drawers. And if you wouldn't mind leaving the door unlocked, it would save us some time." It never happens that way, does it?

Suppose that thieves have been working your neighborhood. How would you protect yourself against them?

- Lock the doors.
- Close the windows.
- Set the burglar alarm.

- Call the security service.
- Get a hungry Doberman.

You might even buy a double-barreled shotgun so you can give the burglars a personal greeting. Now after you do all that, the burglars probably won't come for many nights. In fact, you'll probably not need those precautions for 999 days. But on Day 1,000, you'll be glad you were ready.

Jesus is coming like a thief in the night. When we least expect him, he will return to the earth. Therefore, keep your eyes on the skies and be ready at any moment to meet the Lord face to face.

That leads me to ask a simple question: When was the last time you got up and said to yourself, "Jesus may come today"? For most of us, it's been a long time since we thought about his return. We're not ready because we're not sure he's really coming back.

Fact #4: While We Wait, We Are to Be Faithful in Doing the Tasks the Lord Has Given Us

"Who then is the faithful and wise servant, whom the master has put in charge of the servants in his household to give them their food at the proper time? It will be good for that servant whose master finds him doing so when he returns. I tell you the truth, he will put him in charge of all his possessions. But suppose that servant is wicked and says to himself, 'My master is staying away a long time,' and he then begins to beat his fellow servants and to eat and drink with drunkards. The master of that servant will come on a day when he does not expect him and at an hour he is not aware of. He will cut him to pieces and assign him a place with the hypocrites, where there will be weeping and gnashing of teeth" (Matt. 24:45–51).

Jesus uses the word *faithful* to describe the proper attitude of his followers while we wait for his return. Then he told a most instructive story. There once was a rich man who owned a vast estate. Before he left, he appointed one of his servants to run the estate while he was gone. That man was to handle all the money and oversee all the other servants until the master returned from his journey. He didn't say how long he would be gone, only that one day he would return.

It turned out that the master was gone for a long, long time—much longer than anyone expected. But the servant he put in charge kept saying to himself, "My master is coming back some day—it might be today. I've got to keep things running well so my master will be pleased when he does return." One day the master did come back, saw that his servant had been faithful, and gave him a vast reward.

But suppose the servant didn't believe the master or suppose he believed at first and then lost hope because the master was gone so long? Days become weeks, weeks become months, months become years, and years become decades. Finally the servant says to himself, "My master is never coming back. He lied to me or he forgot or he changed his mind. Maybe he never meant to come back at all. Maybe it was just a story he told to keep me busy." So the servant begins to beat the other workers, he starts drinking and carousing and spending the master's money. After all, the master's been away for two thousand years. How serious can he be about coming back?

But one day—sudden and unannounced—the master returns, and this time there will be no reward. When he sees how the wicked servant had doubted his word, he orders him cast out of the house and cut into pieces. He was no different from the hypocrites and unbelievers.

So it will be when Jesus returns. Those who remain faithful will be rewarded; those who doubt his word and squander their opportunities will be greatly punished.[22]

How can you be ready for Christ's return? Some Christians have answered that question by selling their goods and moving to the wilderness to wait for the Lord. However, Jesus never calls his followers to do such a thing. Instead, he calls us to be faithful in doing whatever he gives us to do.

Your job may be big or small, but whatever it is, do it to the best of your ability and you'll be ready when Jesus returns.

- Be faithful today and you'll be ready today.
- Be faithful tomorrow and you'll be ready tomorrow.
- Be faithful next week and you'll be ready next week.
- Be faithful next year and you'll be ready next year.

A Christian leader was once asked what he would do if he knew Jesus were coming back tomorrow. "I would plant an acorn today," he replied. That's exactly the point. Just keep on doing what you know to be right, and whenever Jesus comes, you won't be disappointed.

Here is the biblical balance for all of us as we await the return of the Lord:

- Live as though he might come today.
- Plan as though he won't return for a thousand years.

Back to the Main Question

As we come to the end of this chapter, you may feel that I've not answered the main question: When is Jesus coming back? Well, if you wanted a date, I can't give you one. Any date I gave would almost certainly be wrong. And to be completely truthful, it's not that I'm hiding a date. I don't know when Jesus will return. I hope he comes soon. He might come in the next five minutes or the next five years or the next fifty years or the next five hundred years. He might come today.

I do know this: Jesus will return when everything is ready in God's plan. Matthew 24 teaches us that there are many different things that will happen in the days leading up to Christ's return. Those signs are like the little streams that lead into the big river that I mentioned earlier. When everything is in place according to God's plan, Jesus will return. Not a moment earlier, not a second later.

How close are we to that moment? Perhaps very close. Certainly closer than we think.

Seven Signs of the Last Days

Let me wrap up this chapter by sharing with you seven signs that lead me to believe we may be living in the last days before the return of Jesus Christ to the earth.

1. *Fig tree blossoming: Israel in the land since 1948.* In my mind this is the most important prophetic event of the last century. After two thousand years the Jewish people are back in their own land.

2. *The rapid move toward a united Europe.* We used to talk about the Common Market; now we speak of eurodollars, a united currency, a European Parliament, and the establishment of a united European trading bloc. This seems to correspond with the prophecies of Daniel 2; Daniel 7; and Revelation 13.

3. *World attention focused on the Middle East.* I simply point out that the Bible clearly tells us that history both begins and ends in the Middle East—not in Africa, Asia, Russia, Europe, or North America.

4. *Global computer/communications network.* The whole trend toward globalization seems to be leading to a situation where one person could control world communication and ultimately the entire world economy, as predicted in Revelation 13.

5. *Vast spiritual apostasy.* Second Timothy 3:1–9 tells us that in the last days "terrible times" will come with people becoming lovers of pleasure instead of lovers of God. They will turn away from the truth because their minds are depraved. False teachers who cleverly counterfeit the truth will lead many others astray. Truly those terrible days are upon us—both in America and around the world. So-called ministers of the gospel deny every tenet of the Christian faith and still remain in the pulpit. They can even justify gross immorality because they have rejected God's Word. The worst is yet to come.

6. *Worldwide preaching of the gospel.* Here is one positive sign. Matthew 24:14 predicts the worldwide preaching of the gospel in the last days. In this generation more people are preaching the gospel in more places with greater results than ever before.

7. *Growing movement of political correctness.* This includes the mania for multiculturalism and the increasing enshrinement of "tolerance" as the chief American virtue. In the name of "tolerance" we attack those who proclaim absolute truth, which is why persecution of Christians is on the increase around the world. I would include in this final sign the ecumenical movement and the willingness of many people—including some evangelicals—to sacrifice truth on the altar of peace and friendship. These things are simply setting us up for the rise of the one final great world ruler whom the Bible calls "the man of lawlessness," "the antichrist," and "the beast" (2 Thess. 2:3; 1 John 2:18; Rev. 13).

"Maybe Today. Are You Ready?"

All these things are happening in the world today, and I would suggest that all of them are signs of the last days. However, that is as far as I am willing to go. I do not know when Christ will return, but I hope and pray that it will be soon. It seems to me that many of the pieces are in place, the table is set, and we are not far from the moment when the curtain will rise on the final act of human history.

Earlier in this chapter I commented on Jesus' use of the budding of the fig tree as a symbol of how events will unfold in the last days before the return of Christ. He applied the truth this way: "When you see all these things, you know that it is near, right at the door" (Matt. 24:33). How much clearer can it be? If you look at a tree and see the leaves sprouting, you know that summer is not far away. It may not come for several weeks or even for a month or two, but once you see the leaves, you *know* summer is coming. In the same way, there will be slowly unfolding signs of the return of Jesus Christ. As those things *begin* to happen, you may be sure that the return of the

Lord cannot be far away. By saying it that way, Jesus is encouraging his followers to examine the world in which they live constantly for the gathering signs of his return. Let me make that stronger: Jesus expects his followers to watch for his return.

Matthew 24 seems to indicate that the signs will unfold slowly before us, which is why it is impossible to say exactly how or where a particular world event fits into the prophetic picture. The time frame is too short. We can't see clearly how this or that crisis affects the flow of end-time events. Instead of thinking in terms of days or months when it comes to prophecy, we need to think in terms of years and decades and generations and even centuries. One generation will see one thing beginning; the next sees something else. One generation sees the spread of liberalism among the mainline churches; another sees the rise of communism; yet another witnesses Hitler's failed attempt to exterminate the Jewish race. That same generation witnesses the establishment of the state of Israel. Twenty years later Israel controls Jerusalem. And twenty years after that the world edges toward war in the Persian Gulf. Within a decade, the Internet revolutionizes communications and makes the world a true "global village."

No single generation sees all these things, but over time as the generations come and go, a flow and pattern becomes apparent. Some things that seemed important in one generation pass into insignificance in the next. But other events build on what has already happened to produce that flow and pattern evident to the thoughtful observer of world history.

Jesus may come in my lifetime. I hope he does. I think the signs point in that direction. But he may not come for five hundred years. The precise date is left in the hand of God. Of this much I am sure: Jesus Christ is coming back to the earth. It may be soon. Maybe today. Although I don't know when Jesus is coming, I fully expect that he will return in my lifetime. I'm not looking for the undertaker; I'm looking for the Lord to return from heaven. I don't want to spend any "box time" in the ground; I'm looking for the Lord to return before I die. If I'm wrong about that, I hope my friends won't hold it against me at my funeral service. But if I'm wrong, at least I'm in good company because the apostle Paul expected Jesus to come in his lifetime too. I'd rather be wrong because I expected Christ to return than to think he won't come back for ten thousand years.

Are We Living in the Last Days?

No one knows for sure. But consider these facts:

1. *There is a clear pattern of events laid out in the Bible concerning the last days.* If you put together the various strands of prophetic teaching from the Old and New Testaments, you discover a fairly detailed picture of the end-time landscape—morally, politically, spiritually, militarily, and economically.

2. *There is an amazing similarity between our world and the world the Bible describes at the end of time.* If you doubt that, take your Bible in one hand and the newspaper in the other. See how well they fit together.

3. *If that is true, then we may indeed be the generation privileged to see the coming of Jesus Christ.*

4. *Every sign points in one direction—it won't be long now.*

Let us suppose you attend a play in a great theater. Before the play begins, there is noise, bustle, confusion, movement behind the curtains, the sound of instruments warming up. Ushers seat latecomers; friends greet one another, find their seats, and study the program. Then the lights flicker on and off. The time is at hand. How much longer? No one can say exactly. Before long, the house lights go down, a hush falls, the conductor lifts his baton, the overture begins, and the curtain slowly rises.

Where are we in this sequence at the dawn of the twenty-first century? The curtain is still down, the music has not started, people are still coming in. But I left out one thing: Just before the house lights go down, the noise of the crowd rises to a roar as everyone talks at once. They know the play is about to begin. That, I believe, is where we are. Almost everyone is seated now. The appointed hour is almost here. The noise you hear is the cacophony of voices in the world just before the house lights go down.

Will we live to see the end of all things? Are we the terminal generation? Is it possible that we will hear the shout, the trumpet, and the voice of the archangel? It is very possible. The stage appears to be set for the final act of human history.

How Should We Then Live?

If that is true, what sort of people should we be? What difference should it make if we believe that we are living in the last days?

1. *We ought to be good students of culture and history.* Not like those who constantly scan the papers looking for the final clue to the prophetic puzzle. But instead, watching for a pattern, a rising tempo, the slow unfolding of end-time events. Francis Schaeffer reminded us that there is a flow to history and culture. Unless we see that, the lessons of history are lost to us.

2. *We ought to live with zeal and enthusiasm.* The message of the coming of Christ ought to fill us with tremendous excitement. These are great days to be alive. We ought to say to one another, "Go for it." This is no time to put off living for God. It is a day to be fully committed, fully engaged, fully involved, aggressively serving the Lord. This is no time to play it safe.

3. *We ought to take an inventory of the way we've been living.* Often people say, "If I knew Jesus were coming tomorrow, I would _____," and they list the changes they would make. But one day it will be true. Therefore, we ought to live that way today.

4. *We ought to face the future with optimism.* The world looks at all the problems and says, "Is there any hope?" For those who know Jesus Christ, there is enormous hope. If he comes today, we win. If

he comes in fifty years, we win. If he comes in a thousand years, we win.

Great Days to Be Alive

These are great days to be alive, the greatest days in all human history. Think of it: We may well be the generation privileged to see the return of Jesus Christ.

- If that is true, there's never been a better time to be a Christian.
- If that is true, there's never been a better time to tell someone else.
- If that is true, there's never been a better time to raise a Christian family.

One final word: If it is true that we are the terminal generation, then we will see increasingly scary things in the days ahead:

- diseases worse than AIDS,
- nuclear blackmail on every hand,
- further breakdown of the home,
- precipitous decline in moral standards, and
- false Christs who will lead many astray.

As the Bible says, perilous times will come. But in this we have the words of Jesus—"See to it that you are not alarmed" (Matt. 24:6).

The bottom line is quite simple: If Jesus comes today, will you be ready? If he comes tomorrow, will you be ready? If he comes in your lifetime, will you be ready?

If this really is the terminal generation, the smartest thing you can do is to give your life 100 percent to Jesus Christ so that if he comes today or tomorrow or next week or next year or in a hundred years, you will have no regrets but will be ready to see him when he returns.

Jesus is coming again. Maybe today. Are you ready?

A Truth to Remember:
Jesus will return when everything is ready in God's plan.

Going Deeper

1. Why has the Second Coming of Christ always been considered a fundamental Christian doctrine? What happens when this truth is denied, ignored, or minimized?
2. Why did Jesus compare the days of Noah with the days preceding his return to the earth? In what ways is the present generation like the generation that watched Noah build the ark?
3. Do you believe Christ will return in your own lifetime? Why or why not? Why is it dangerous to set a date for Christ's return?
4. "Jesus is coming. Are you ready?" How would you answer that question? If you knew that Jesus was returning tomorrow, how would you spend the next twenty-four hours?
5. Think for a moment of your family and closest friends. What is their relationship to Jesus Christ? What will happen to them when Christ returns?
6. Of the seven "signs" of the Second Coming listed in this chapter, which ones seem most significant to you?

Taking Action

Think of a friend or loved one who does not know Christ. Write a letter sharing what you believe about the Second Coming of Christ and why you hope he (or she) will trust Christ as Savior. If you are doing this in a group, share your letters with one another. If you feel comfortable doing so, mail the letter accompanied by fervent prayers that God will use it to bring your friend or loved one to Christ.

A FINAL WORD

Where to from here? If this book is basic training, then once you finish it, you are ready for the next step. Before you go further, remember that the Christian life is a journey that starts on earth and ends in heaven. It begins the moment you trust Christ as Savior and doesn't end until you pass through the gates of heaven. Between now and then you will have good days and bad days, and lots of in-between days. Those up-and-down times aren't bad if you keep in mind the things we have talked about in this book. God has a purpose for your life that he is working out moment by moment. He has a plan for you, and he has given you special talents to help you fulfill that plan.

Years ago I heard a Bible teacher say that the Christian life can be reduced to a simple formula: T + HH = SG. I'm not much for formulas, but this one has always made sense to me. T stands for *Time*. No one becomes a mature Christian overnight. If you have struggled with bad habits, you will probably continue to struggle with them for some time to come. As you grow in Christ, some sins will have less power in your life while others may be a challenge as long as you live. Take time to learn God's Word, to listen to the Holy Spirit, to develop deep friendships, to discover your spiritual gifts, and to find ways to serve others. Be sure you take time to worship God individually and with other believers. Even if you are a senior adult, don't rush the Lord. Give him time to grow your faith.

HH stands for *Habits of Holiness*. Habits are those things we do by nature because we have done them so many times before. Habits of Holiness would include Scripture memory, learning to sing God's praises through hymns and choruses, reading the Bible every day, recording how God answers your prayers, and meeting regularly with other believers for worship and instruction in God's Word. It also includes learning to give generously to support God's work through your local church and through other Christian ministries. For most of us it also includes having a few close Christian friends who can encourage us with wise counsel and a cheerful smile. And it certainly involves learning how to share your faith with others.

That list is suggestive, not exhaustive. It illustrates how Time plus Habits of Holiness eventually produces genuine *Spiritual Growth*. There are no shortcuts in the Christian life. But there is a way all of us can eventually become strong in our faith. Every soldier knows that you win a war by fighting a series of battles, and you win a battle by fighting a series of skirmishes in many places. And every soldier will tell you that what happens before the battle begins determines who is standing victorious at the end of the day.

Basic training is over. Now it's time to go into battle. God has given you everything you need to succeed as a Christian. The next step is up to you.

Special Note

If you would like to contact the author, you can reach him in the following ways:

By Letter: Ray Pritchard
                    Calvary Memorial Church
                    931 Lake Street
                    Oak Park, IL 60301

By E-mail: PastorRay@calvarymemorial.com

Via the Internet: www.calvarymemorial.com

NOTES

1. *Newsweek* poll conducted by Princeton Survey Research Associates. April 13–14, 2000.

2. The Harris Poll. July 17–21, 1998.

3. Gallup/CNN/*USA Today* Poll. March 17–19, 2000.

4. Dr. Graham gave this illustration during his sermon on March 17, 1995, in the Global Mission Crusade broadcast from Puerto Rico.

5. John Piper makes this point in his sermon "Fear of God, Freedom from Goods," December 2, 1990.

6. I believe Jesus is trying to get the man to see that his money was standing between him and God. His money had become an idol and until he tore down the idol (by giving his money away to the poor), he could never see his true need of salvation.

7. Walt Gerber, "One Incredible Way to Love," sermon delivered March 15–16, 1997.

8. Ray Stedman develops this concept in his sermon "Prayer's Certainties," March 22, 1964.

9. Portions of this chapter first appeared as an article in *Moody Magazine*, "From Temptation to Triumph," March/April 1998.

10. Haddon Robinson, "God Still Expects Sexual Purity," *Good News Broadcaster* (May 1996), 35.

11. James Montgomery Boice, *Genesis,* vol. III (Grand Rapids: Zondervan, 1987), 61.

12. Franklin Graham and Jeannette Lockerbie, *This One Thing I Do* (Nashville: Word Books, 1983).

13. The information in this paragraph comes from urban missiologist Ray Bakke.

14. Wilbur M. Smith, *Therefore Stand* (Grand Rapids: Baker Book House, 1976 reprint), 248.

15. One recent example would be the Harris Poll conducted July 17–21, 1998. It reported that 89 percent of those surveyed believe in heaven, and 76 percent expect to go there.

16. There have been many books and articles written in recent years about heaven based on dreams, visions, and near-death experiences. The majority of these should be rejected because they contain bad theology. Having said that, I do not doubt that some believers have had genuine experiences with angels and have been given a glimpse of heaven. But wonderful as those stories may be, I do not think we should build our theology around them.

17. Three times the writer of Hebrews uses a Greek word that means "to come near" or "to approach closely."

18. I mean by this that heaven includes the Old Testament saints who by faith trusted in God's Word and looked forward to God's redemption at Calvary (which they did not fully understand). It also includes every true believer from every continent and every denomination. Everyone who has genuinely trusted in Christ as Lord and Savior will be there. I also think that children who died before the "age of accountability" go to heaven, and I would also include those born with such mental limitations that they cannot understand the gospel.

19. William Pettingill and R. A. Torrey, *1001 Bible Questions Answered* (New York: Inspirational Press, 1997), 157.

20. "Dark Prophecies," *U.S. News and World Report*, 15 December 1997. The *Newsweek* poll was taken October 21–22, 1999.

21. The statement that not even the Son knows the date of his return (v. 36) means that as a man Jesus voluntarily laid aside the divine knowledge of when he would return to the earth. As God he certainly knew the date; as man he chose not to know it—possibly to serve as an example for us who also do not know the date of his return. Upon his return to heaven that voluntary self-limitation was no longer necessary.

22. Some have wondered if this passage teaches that true believers can lose their salvation. There is some debate among the commentators as to who the "wicked servant" represents. Given the severe nature of the punishment and given that he is apportioned a place with the hypocrites, I take it that this servant represents a person who is religious but lost. He claims to believe in Jesus, but since he doesn't believe in his return, his lifestyle manifests the unregenerate state of his heart.